Monsters

AND

Mythical Creatures

FROM AROUND THE WORLD

HEATHER FRIGIOLA

ILLUSTRATED BY SKY CYBELE

REDFeather™

MIND | BODY | SPIRIT

4880 Lower Valley Road, Atglen, PA 19310

Designed by Jack Chappell
Cover design by Jack Chappell
Type set in Affair/Trajan/Adobe Caslon Pro
ISBN: 978-0-7643-5842-5
Printed in China

Published by Red Feather Mind, Body, Spirit
An imprint of Schiffer Publishing, Ltd.
4880 Lower Valley Road
Atglen, PA 19310
Phone: (610) 593-1777; Fax: (610) 593-2002
E-mail: Info@schifferbooks.com
Web: www.redfeathermbs.com

For our complete selection of fine books on this and related subjects, please visit our website at www.schifferbooks.com. You may also write for a free catalog.

Schiffer Publishing's titles are available at special discounts for bulk purchases for sales promotions or premiums. Special editions, including personalized covers, corporate imprints, and excerpts, can be created in large quantities for special needs. For more information, contact the publisher.

We are always looking for people to write books on new and related subjects. If you have an idea for a book, please contact us at proposals@schifferbooks.com.

Contents

Introduction

THE IMPORTANCE OF
MYTHICAL CREATURES

Myth is a vital part of human existence all around the world. Many scholars draw a technical distinction between myths, legends, and folktales, yet all three categories are products of the same universal human behavior. *Homo sapiens* are dreamers and storytellers. As such, we use symbols to express abstract ideas and share our interpretations of the world around us. Whether a myth is intended to explain a real phenomenon or simply to entertain, all stories have the potential to leave a cultural imprint for generations to come.

In this book, mythical creatures are treated as cultural artifacts. As with any tool or work of art, mythical creatures are creations of the human imagination that have a distinctive form and meaning. The meanings of mythical creatures vary case by case. Some symbolize obstacles that must be overcome, while others are prizes to be sought. Some are bogey monsters used for scaring children. Some explain the occurrence of diseases and misfortune. Some are demonized caricatures of foreign enemies. Some mythical creatures are benevolent guardians, protectors that ward away evil, and bringers of prosperity. Some are associated with the gods and important spiritual events. Some are believed to be real, and others are created for amusement.

Whatever their meaning, all mythical creatures are expressions of human culture. For this reason, this book focuses on their cultural origin and context. Myths evolve over time, and a mythical creature is defined by its history within a culture's folklore. When one culture adopts another culture's myths, the meaning of the creatures inevitably changes. Today, fantasy authors and game developers frequently borrow mythical creatures from around the world and place them in novel contexts. This changes their meaning, yet it also provides an invitation for fantasy fans to investigate the traditional versions of the myths.

This book is intended to be an enjoyable, informative resource for anyone who has wondered where fantastical creatures come from. It should be immediately obvious that mythical creatures come from everywhere. They do not come just from ancient Greece and medieval Europe. They come from every part of the world and every time period, including present day. They come from small tribes in the jungle. They come from sprawling modern cities. They come from all societies that produce myth and legend, which means they come from all societies.

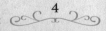

HOW THIS BOOK WAS WRITTEN

Unlike other books that classify mythical creatures on the basis of their supposed biology, this book classifies them by the cultures that created them. The ten chapters are based on major regions of the globe. Ancient Greece and Rome have claimed an entire chapter of their own due to their extensive, monster-filled mythology, which is highly popular in the West. Other chapters are assigned to large geographic areas. Each chapter features twenty-four different mythical beasts, which is merely a sampling. Every region will easily yield many more upon further research.

One challenge in writing this book was to decide what qualifies as a mythical creature. Not every mythological being is a "creature." For instance, some mythological beings are gods or goddesses. Deities are divine, are usually human-like in appearance, and are defined by their worship, whereas creatures are not. Some entries in this book approach a blurred line between the two. These represent beasts that were believed to be divine, including shapeshifted forms of gods. Yet, out of respect for the religious beliefs of different cultures past and present, beings conventionally included in official pantheons are not listed here as "creatures."

Mythical creatures are also distinguished from other beings by their fantastical form. In this book, beings qualifying as mythical creatures always look different from humans and ordinary animals. Some are humanoid in their overall shape but will have certain unusual or grotesque features. Certain famous mythical beings, such as Baba Yaga from Russia and La Llorona from Mexico, are excluded from this bestiary because their appearance is fully human. In some cases the word "monster" appears in this book, although it is not clearly defined. Oftentimes this word implies a mythical creature that is terrifying and unpleasant. However, popular culture frequently portrays benevolent monsters as well.

This bestiary is not and was never intended to be a complete list of all the world's mythical creatures. It would literally be impossible to write a book that includes every monster of myth. There are easily thousands of mythical creatures in all the world's known myths, while innumerable others have been forgotten by time. It was difficult to narrow the list down to the 240 that would fit into this volume. Any monster enthusiast will surely be able to name many creatures that do not appear in this book, yet they will just as surely also learn something new.

A MESSAGE FOR MYTH SEEKERS

This book encourages readers to think more critically about the world. For every instance that you see a mythical creature taken out of its original context, think about how its story is being changed. Think about the new myths being created and what parts of the old myths are being left behind. Did the creature come from Western civilization originally, or Eastern civilization, or an indigenous society? Is there cultural appropriation involved? How much do you think the media creator understood about the original myth and the culture that imagined it?

Take notice of cultural appropriation and Eurocentrism in English-language fantasy. Westerners often interpret the myths of other cultures through a Eurocentric lens without intending to do so. For instance, some sources claim that dragons appear in myths throughout the world. In actuality, there are giant serpents and other reptiles throughout world myth, yet only the European and East Asian forms are properly called dragons. Likewise, some sources identify all immortal birds as phoenixes and all parasitic humanoids as vampires. When this happens, the mythical creature's uniqueness and relevance to its original culture is being erased and replaced with the folklore of Europe.

Similar problems can occur in cryptozoology. Developed in the 1950s by the Belgian zoologist Bernard Heuvelmans, cryptozoology was originally intended to be the scientific search for new species of animals. It was not intended to be the study of mythical creatures. However, in practice, the distinction is often blurred. Many cryptozoology enthusiasts adopt and reclassify traditional mythical creatures as cryptids. In particular, they often target myths from indigenous societies, speculating that their fantastic monsters are real animals, unlike the monsters of Greek myths. This disparity suggests that Westerners do not regard the imaginations of indigenous peoples as truly imaginative. Despite their innocent intentions, they perpetuate a colonialist view of mythmaking from non-Western cultures.

The fact is that humans are universally mythmaking beings, and this is as true for us today as it was thousands of years ago. Fantasy is mythology. Cryptozoology is mythology. Most importantly, myth has merit! As rumored sightings of strange creatures persist in fringe media, even the belief in their existence remains alive. The industrialized world is no different from tribal society in this regard: we all love our monsters. Every culture is unique, yet all of them share this in common. For every mythical creature you encounter, think of it as an expression of the culture that created it. Embrace your own interest in myth. Integrate what you learn about other cultures and expand your own mythology. Keep on seeking.

Chapter One

NORTH AMERICA

In this chapter, "North America" refers to the United States of America, Canada, and Greenland. Despite being only three countries, this region is extraordinarily diverse. It is home to hundreds of millions of English speakers of European descent, as well as African diaspora, French Canadians, Spanish speakers, and immigrants from all over the world. This continent is also the birthplace of indigenous peoples who arrived 14,000 years ago or longer. Over this time these First Nations developed extensive trade networks and diverse societies from coast to coast. The US and Canadian governments recognize about 1,200 different tribes and groups.

The majority of the mythical creatures in this chapter are associated with these First Nations. Obviously, some twenty creatures represent just a tiny sample of their mythology. Regardless, the creatures in this chapter provide insight on the worldviews of Native American cultures, including how they differ from Euro-American culture, and from one another. Mythical creatures have also appeared spontaneously among the societies of non-Native North Americans. For instance, lumberjacks have produced a robust mythical corpus with monsters known as Fearsome Critters. In addition, some mythical creatures have become iconic symbols of specific regions. Certain ones are regarded as cryptids today. These myths and legends illustrate the elaborate, ever-evolving history of cultural blending that characterizes the North American people.

ADLET

The adlets are a malevolent group of half-dog, half-humanoid monsters from Inuit mythology. They are the descendants of a woman who married a dog. Adlets have human-like upper bodies and the legs of dogs, which enable them to run extremely fast. They are also taller than most humans. They appear in folklore from Greenland, Hudson Bay, and the Labrador coast. Stories of a woman being impregnated by a dog are also told in Alaskan folklore.

The most famous story about the adlet was recorded in Baffin Land in the 1880s. The myth is a cautionary tale about a woman who refuses to marry a man. According to legend, a young woman named Niviarsiang married a dog named Ijirqang.

The dog could not provide for her, so they lived with the woman's father, Savirqong. Niviarsiang gave birth to ten children. Five of them looked like normal dogs and five were adlets. Savirqong quickly tired of housing his daughter's monstrous brood, so he sent them all to live on a small island. The dog had to swim across the water in order to retrieve food from his father-in-law. He would carry a pair of boots around his neck, which Savirqong would fill up with meat. One day Savirqong filled the boots with rocks, causing the dog to sink and drown. Enraged, Niviarsiang gathered her children and crossed the water in a boat. She sent the adlets to attack her father, whereupon they chewed off his hands and feet. Then she sent the adlet children off into the wilderness, where they dispersed. Today their descendants continue to roam and prey on humans.

BIGFOOT

—See *Sasquatch*.

DEER WOMAN

Deer, especially female deer, symbolize fertility and sexuality among many First Nations. Traditionally this was seen in a positive light. In some tribes' folklore, Deer Woman helps women conceive children. Yet, for some southeastern US tribes, such as the Cherokee and Creek, Deer Woman is a sinister temptress who brings doom to young men. Above the waist she is a doe-eyed woman, and below the waist she has the legs of a deer. She is capable of appearing fully human.

While in disguise, Deer Woman will often join community dances. Usually the whole village is unaware of her intrusion, yet if somebody takes a good, direct look at her feet, they will notice she has hooves. Once one person recognizes Deer Woman for what she is, her disguise ceases to be effective and she runs off into the woods. Deer Woman always vanishes into the spirit realm after leaving the community dances; therefore no man is able to have her. Some men succumb hopelessly to her charm and waste away from obsession and despair.

In some contemporary versions of the myth, Deer Woman stands behind a bush with her animal legs concealed and lures young men over to join her. If the man allows his desires to get the better of him, she will stomp him to death with her hooves. Among the tribes relocated to Oklahoma, some say Deer Woman is the vengeful ghost of a woman who was murdered. Parents may warn their children that she will come and get them if they misbehave. These negative interpretations are most likely of recent origin, as Deer Woman was historically considered sacred.

HODAG

The hodag belongs to a category of North American mythical creatures known as Fearsome Critters. These monsters are the subject of campfire stories told by lumberjacks and other outdoorsmen. Having since expanded beyond the context of campfire entertainment, the hodag has become the official mascot of the town of

Rhinelander, Wisconsin. Today there are local sports teams named the Hodags, an annual Hodag Country Music Festival, and a large fiberglass hodag sculpture in front of the Rhinelander chamber of commerce. A popular black-and-white postcard depicts the hodag as a mere dog-sized beast standing on a log, cornering a terrified boy. Behind it are some two dozen angry townsmen with their pitchforks raised at the creature.

Varying descriptions of the hodag have appeared in early-twentieth-century books about Fearsome Critters. The most well-known account claims it was discovered by a naturalist named Eugene Shepard in 1896, as he passed by a lumber camp in Rhinelander. There stood the gigantic beast, allegedly having emerged from a pile of ashes where expired oxen were being cremated. Shepard described it as a composite of many animals, with the back of a dinosaur lined with spikes, and thick, short claws on its four massive feet. It had two large horns on its head, tusks, and a long tail ending in a spear-like point. Shepard instructed the lumberjacks to dig a pit that was 50 feet across and bait it with an ox. Once the hodag fell in, they put it to sleep by using a chloroform-soaked sponge on the end of a 30-foot-long pole. Finally they killed it using dynamite.

HORNED SERPENT

The horned serpent is one of the most ubiquitous classes of monsters in First Nations mythology. There are tribes that tell stories of horned serpents in nearly every corner of North America except the Arctic. Conceptions of these serpents inevitably vary from culture to culture, yet there are a number of common themes that recur across vast geographic distances. The horned serpent is typically very large in size. It usually dwells in water. In eastern regions it is the enemy of the thunderbird. The horned serpent is always powerful and potentially dangerous and is sometimes portrayed as malevolent. In most tribes it is a complex sacred being that is neither good nor evil.

Among the Lakota, the horned serpent is called Unktehi. The male Unktehi dwell in the water and the females on land; they are known as sacred water and earth spirits, respectively. The Cherokee horned serpent has a similar name, Uktena, although the stories about it are much different. Uktena is a fierce and vengeful beast. His body is covered with glittery, fiery scales, and he has a magical jewel on his forehead. Called the *ulunsuti*, this jewel causes people to run toward the serpent, who then kills them. This jewel is an object sought by questing heroes. Among the Pueblo peoples of the Southwest, the horned serpent is associated with fertility and is generally regarded in a positive light. The Yurok of Northern California tell multiple stories of a man who adopted a juvenile horned serpent as a pet. It brings him good fortune until his family forces him to abandon his pet in the wilderness.

HVCKO-CAPKO

Hvcko-Capko is a repugnant animal from Seminole folklore. The Seminole people originated in Florida, yet today most of them live in Oklahoma. Hvcko-Capko is therefore associated with the Panhandle State. Occasionally, people have reported sightings of this ominous creature, even in recent times. It is typically described as wolf-like or wolf-headed, with a horse tail and deer legs. Yet, descriptions are not all consistent with each other, and it seems Hvcko-Capko has become the default explanation for any animal that is difficult to identify. Its size is said variously to be either 3 feet tall, or as large as a donkey, or potentially larger than that. It is ugly and gray in color, with long legs, as well as large eyes that enable it to see in the dark. Hvcko-Capko is sometimes said to have long ears that hang down like a basset hound's. Its name means "Long Ears." It is pronounced "Hutcko" Capko; the letter *v* makes an "uh" sound in the Muskogean languages.

Belief in Hvcko-Capko may have originated sometime after the Indian Removal Act of 1830. The US government continued to attack the Seminoles in a series of wars until all of them were forced out of their Florida homeland. The beast may be a metaphor for the misery faced by the Seminoles as they were banished to what was then the frontier. Hvcko-Capko is not aggressive toward humans, yet attitudes toward it are negative. This cryptid dwells in a rocky habitat and can be detected by its odor, a foul stench that reeks like stagnant swamp. It also carries disease and causes people to fall ill. Its presence is a sign of misfortune.

JACKALOPE

An icon of the American West, the jackalope is a cross between a jackrabbit and a pronghorn antelope. Oftentimes it is portrayed as having the antlers of a deer rather than the horns of an antelope. This creature of modern-day folklore fits in among the Fearsome Critters of woodsmen's campfire tales, although its origin was somewhat different. Two brothers named Ralph and Doug Herrick, from Douglas, Wyoming, claimed to have created the first jackalope in 1934 in their taxidermy shop. They spontaneously came up with the idea to mount antlers onto a stuffed rabbit after placing a dead rabbit next to a pair of antlers. Their impromptu creation became instantly popular. The Herricks assembled and sold hundreds of jackalopes that became distributed throughout the country. A company in South Dakota later began producing the novelty creatures after the Herricks retired from taxidermy.

It became widely held that the jackalope is a wily trickster, usually not aggressive, yet dangerous if cornered. It will imitate various animal sounds, including human voices, in order to deceive hunters. This species originated from the mating of an antelope and rabbit. Jackalopes can also reproduce with their own kind, yet they are only able to breed during storms that have lightning and hail. To most Americans this legendary creature is not tied to any one specific locale. Nonetheless, Douglas, Wyoming, maintains that it is the birthplace of the mythical American icon. The city's chamber of commerce distributes jackalope-related material to tourists, including novelty hunting permits. These permits only allow jackalope hunting within the county on one day of the year, June 31.

JERSEY DEVIL

The Jersey Devil, or Leeds Devil, is a folk monster from a wooded region of New Jersey called the Pine Barrens. It has become one of the most famous monsters in Anglo-American folklore. The legend dates back to at least the early nineteenth century and is said to be even older than this. Hundreds and possibly thousands of eyewitness sightings have been reported over the years, compelling some paranormal enthusiasts to believe that the creature is an existing unknown entity. Although descriptions vary, it is usually said to have leathery wings, a head like a horse or ram, and a long, thin tail. It produces a blood-chilling cry that can be heard deep in the woods at night. This monster has also been blamed for killing livestock. The vast majority of sightings took place in January 1909.

The most popular legend explaining the origin of the Jersey Devil concerns a woman called Mother Leeds. This story is usually said to take place in 1735. Mother Leeds had given birth to twelve children and did not want to have any more. Upon her thirteenth pregnancy she said, "This one could be the devil!" In some versions it was born a monster; in others it looked normal at first and then quickly changed its shape. This "devil" terrorized the town until it was banished by an exorcist. It did not return until a century later. In one version of the story, the mother's name was Leeds, and she lived in Estelville, New Jersey. In another, her name was Shrouds, and she lived in Leeds Point. Others identify Burlington as the monster's birthplace.

KOKOGIAK

The kokogiak is a legendary ten-legged polar bear, also spelled *qupqugiaq*. It is known from Inupiat Inuit mythology. When this bear walks, it moves its feet in unison. It steps into its own paw prints, leaving tracks that are indistinguishable from those of four-legged bears. The kokogiak is portrayed varyingly as dreadful or beneficent, or both at the same time. It will kill a person just as any other polar bear will. Yet, in addition to being a predator, it can also be a spirit animal helper. This particular spirit animal is normally restricted to shamans, who are able to ride on the creature's back. Some Inupiats believe ordinary polar bears turn into kokogiaks when they become a shaman's spirit helper.

Once there was a man named Kucirak. There was very little food that winter, and his family was extremely hungry. Another family lived nearby. They had some food but refused to share it. Kucirak went out hunting for seals, when the dreaded kokogiak popped its head up through the hole in the ice. Quickly Kucirak speared out its eyes. The blinded kokogiak chased after him by his scent. Kucirak ran through a gap between two walls of ice, causing the kokogiak to become trapped. Kucirak was then able to kill it with his spear. Unbeknown to him, the act of catching a kokogiak would bring him good fortune. The selfish neighbors started showing compassion to Kucirak's family. All of them then went out to butcher the kokogiak together. The beast was as large as a whale and provided both families with enough food to last them through the winter.

MOTHMAN

Mothman is a paranormal monster of recent origin, based in Point Pleasant, West Virginia. The first Mothman sighting took place on November 15, 1966. Four people driving past an abandoned TNT factory alleged that their car was pursued by a winged humanoid monster. They could not see it clearly in the darkness, and they could not see its head. All they could discern of its face were glowing red eyes, which were positioned below where they thought its shoulders should be.

After they reported their sighting to the local newspaper, other people began reporting similar sightings. Descriptions were fairly consistent with one another. Journalists came to dub it "Mothman," as a joking reference to Batman, although the creature was never said to look like a moth. Some people wondered if the creature was a mutant connected to the goings-on of the TNT factory. Reports persisted for about a year.

Suddenly, the town became distracted by the collapse of the Silver Bridge crossing the Ohio River. The bridge collapse resulted in forty-six deaths and was declared a national tragedy. Mothman sightings ceased, yet the legend continued to escalate for years later. People later began to say Mothman was seen on or near the bridge shortly before its collapse. The creature also came to be associated with poltergeist activity and UFO sightings. The Mothman enigma has brought folklore and tourist appeal to the small town. A statue of the creature, detailed with antennae and other insect-like features, was erected in 2003. Point Pleasant also has a Mothman Museum and holds an annual Mothman Festival.

PALRAIYUK

The palraiyuk, or Pal Rai Yuk, is an unusual mythical creature from western Alaska. The Yupiks believe it to be extinct today, yet in ancient times its species was allegedly numerous near the Yukon and the Kuksokwim Rivers. The Yupiks claim the climate of that area used to be warmer and had shorter winters. Images of the palraiyuk were traditionally painted on boats and wooden dishes and have been found on artifacts as far west as St. Lawrence Island.

The amphibious palraiyuk thrived in the grassy marshes between the two waters. It had a long, serpentine body with three humps. Each hump bore a dorsal fin and a pair of legs. The chimerical beast was evidently a mammal, as it was also said to be covered in short, thick, dark-colored fur. It was an alpha predator possessing remarkably long jaws filled with sharp teeth and was known to prey on humans. The last palraiyuk was supposedly killed by a man who lost his wife to the beast. The Yupik also believe these animals declined upon the arrival of the Europeans.

Aside from its peculiar physical qualities, the palraiyuk is also remarkable because of its known antiquity. With many First Nations mythical creatures, it is difficult to determine whether or not the myths predate the arrival of Western culture. Some scholars had presumed the palraiyuk to be a postcolonial invention. Westerners frequently compared the creature to an alligator or crocodile, or even a dinosaur, any of which would have been unknown to native Alaskan societies prior to outside influence. However, artifacts depicting the palraiyuk have been discovered at sites predating Western contact by hundreds of years.

PAMOLA

Pamola is a majestic supernatural being known in the state of Maine. In modern times he is depicted as having the head of a moose and the wings of an eagle. His torso is usually rendered as humanoid, although often covered with feathers, and his hands and feet are like an eagle's claws. This distinctive creature appears on numerous insignia throughout the Katahdin region of Maine. Mount Katahdin, where Pamola is believed to reside, has a peak named after him. Pamola is also the mascot of Baxter State Park, where the mountain is located. The Boy Scouts of America have a Katahdin-based honor camping society known as Pamola Lodge.

The legend of Pamola is credited to the Penobscot Native Americans. This fantastical creature is a sacred, powerful spirit who wields control over snow and thunder. He guards Mt. Katahdin, the tallest mountain in the state, upon which the Penobscot historically refrained from setting foot. Pamola of traditional myth differs considerably from the whimsical creature often depicted in contemporary times. Originally he was described as bird-like rather than moose headed and may have been a type of thunderbird. In the past they believed him to be merciless toward anyone who dared to trespass on the sacred mountain. It was said that he would kill any intruder. In the twentieth century, the myth of Pamola became reinterpreted by a dedicated mountaineer named Leroy Dudley. Pamola was transformed into his contemporary incarnation through the entertaining yarns Dudley told to visitors of Mt. Katahdin. Today this mountain spirit accepts hikers and campers as long as they respect nature.

PIASA

The Piasa is a terrifying monster with wings, scales, and antlers. It has become a historical icon in and around the city of Alton, Illinois. In the seventeenth century, two Native American paintings allegedly depicting this creature were visible high up on a cliff face overlooking the Mississippi River near Alton. The French missionary Jacques Marquette described the animals as being the size of a calf, with four legs, bearded human-like faces, and long tails that circled all the way around their bodies. The paintings were obscured by 1700, yet newer versions were added later. The Piasa came to be imagined as a winged creature, although the original images did not have wings.

In 1836, an Alton seminary professor named John Russell interpreted the monster as an enormous bird. He wrote that this awesome yet horrible bird captures human beings and brings them up to a cave filled with bones. According to Russell, the Piasa Bird was slain by an Illini war chief named Ouatoga. This chief offered himself as a sacrifice to the flying beast while his warriors concealed themselves behind rocks and bushes. When the Piasa appeared, the warriors loosed their arrows. The Illini then painted the monster's image onto the cliff to commemorate their victory.

Scholars have since exposed Russell's Piasa legend as a fabrication of his own imagination. In fact, the Piasa was never a First Nations mythical creature at all. The original paintings are now thought to have depicted the underwater panther. Nonetheless, the Piasa is an important regional icon today. Its image has been continually repainted on the bluff near Alton since 1924.

PUGWIS

Pugwis, also spelled Poogweese, is a sacred water spirit of the Kwakiutl people from the Pacific coast of Canada. He is often described as a merman in English-language sources; however, he does not look like the European idea of a merman. A painting of Pugwis by Chief Lelooska depicts a humanoid-shaped creature covered in fish-like skin, with small fins along his spine, and webbed hands and feet. Traditional Kwakiutl masks portray Pugwis with round, beady eyes and two large front teeth like an otter. He is also said to have long, scraggly hair and is clad in seaweed.

The legend of Pugwis recalls a time when the Kwakiutl were starving. One day Pugwis came up in a fisherman's net. The creature said he was the messenger of Goomaquay, the lord of the wealth of the sea. The fishermen suddenly feared that Goomaquay would punish them if Pugwis were to tell him of his capture. Pugwis then struck up a bargain with the fishermen. He swore that if they released him, he would tell his lord how kind the fishermen were, and Goomaquay would reward them with great bounty.

The fishermen reluctantly let him go. At first they feared they had made a big mistake. Pugwis then sent his mask floating up to the surface and sang his song through the water. All supernatural beings in Kwakiutl belief have masks and songs. The people were then blessed with great harvests, just as Pugwis had promised. The fishermen shared the mask and song with their tribe at a joyous celebration called a potlatch. The Pacific Northwest coast was always bountiful thereafter.

SASQUATCH

The myth of Sasquatch, also popularly known as Bigfoot, is currently alive and thriving. Today there are millions of people throughout the United States and Canada who believe in the existence of this cryptid. This belief is demonstrated and perpetuated by countless sightings, footprints, reports of the creature's chilling cry, a few photographs, and even purported hair samples. Sightings have been reported coast to coast by persons of all demographics. BFRO, the Bigfoot Field Research Organization, has collected 3,313 reported sightings between 1921 and 2013, or approximately thirty to forty per year. Theoretically there are far more sightings than this, as many witnesses fear ridicule or otherwise decline to file a report.

The prevailing theory among believers is that an entire population of sasquatches roams North America, representing a species unknown to science. Some believers speculate it is a surviving population of fossil ape called *Gigantopithecus*. Others suppose it to be something more human-like. The large, bipedal, ape-like humanoids range in height from 6.5 to 9 feet tall or taller. They are covered with black or brown hair, their head is slightly conical, and their noses are flat. Their footprints average between 12 and 20 inches in length, although larger and smaller ones are also reported. The creature is also said to produce a noxious musk when frightened. Skeptics note a lack of physical remains. Believers counter this by suggesting that sasquatches bury their dead deep in the woods. As cryptids go, sasquatch is one of the more zoologically plausible. Nonetheless, it will remain classified as mythical until definitive proof is found.

SEAWOLF

The seawolf is a sacred aquatic beast from the Pacific Northwest coast. The Haida call it Wasco or Waasghu, while the Tlingit call it Gonakadet. A similar creature from Inuit folklore is called Akhlut. This enormous marine animal has a wolf-like head, four limbs with paws, and a dorsal fin. Sometimes it is said to have fangs sticking out of its nostrils, which it uses to kill its prey. The seawolf preys on whales and will sometimes devour humans as well. It is also a shapeshifter. This creature is invisible to humans most of the time, although it may be captured and killed by individuals who have had a close encounter with a spirit being. Today the seawolf is an important symbol of Native culture in the Pacific Northwest. The Tlingit associate it with wealth and prosperity.

In one Haida story, a man lost his brothers to a seawolf. Later this man gained special powers after being tried in combat by a red-skinned, troll-like spirit. He was also visited by a shapeshifter named Mouse Woman, who gave him some magical herbs. Following these encounters, he was able to capture the seawolf in a trap. He attempted to cut the animal open, but lightning immediately struck whenever he pierced its carcass. He made several attempts, eventually finding that it is only safe to slice open from the base of its tail. Finally, he removed the remains of his brothers and smeared them with the magical herbs from Mouse Woman. His brothers came back to life and were extremely thankful. Other tales speak of a hunter donning the seawolf's skin, thus transforming into the creature.

SHUNKA WARAK'IN

The Ioway Native Americans of the northern Midwest provide an account of a beast called the shunka warak'in. Its name means "carries off dogs." There was once a village that kept losing dogs to some unknown visitor in the night. After this problem continued for several nights, the warriors stayed up and waited for the culprit. When the dog thief returned they saw a strange beast they had never seen before. It was vaguely wolf-like, yet not a wolf. The warriors pursued the mysterious animal for a day and a half. It was difficult to kill and said to have cried like a person when it died. Due to the mysterious nature of the shunka warak'in, the villagers decided it must possess great spiritual power. They made sure to preserve its skin and put pieces of it in their medicine bags.

Perhaps the tale of the shunka warak'in would have faded into obscurity if it were not for another case that took place in 1886. A pioneer family by the name of Hutchins shot a strange, dark-colored predator on their Montana ranch. One of the Hutchinses purportedly held a PhD in zoology yet was unable to identify the creature with certainty. They donated the animal to a museum in Idaho, where it was put on display and labeled

 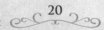

"Ringdocus." Upon viewing the specimen, an Ioway man named Lance Foster said it could be a shunka warak'in. Skeptics believe the taxidermic mount is merely a wolf that was stuffed very poorly, perhaps intentionally, to look like a different animal. Its current owner wants to keep the mystery alive by not submitting samples for DNA testing.

SIDEHILL GOUGER

The sidehill gouger is one of the Fearsome Critters of Anglo-American tall tales. Across different regions it is known by many other names, including the sidehill dodger, sidehill hoofer, sidehill wowser, and gyascutus, although the latter sometimes refers to a different creature. In all cases, the sidehill gouger has short legs on one side of its body and long legs on the other because it dwells on steep hills and mountains. Its appearance is usually compared to a deer or other hoofed mammal. The name "gouger" comes from the fact that it creates a noticeable groove in the soil as it repeatedly circles about the hill while grazing.

Unlike other hoofed animals, the sidehill gouger lives in burrows. It also lays eggs. Most descriptions imply that the species can only travel in one direction. When a clockwise specimen encounters a counterclockwise specimen, they fight with one another. The loser is sent rolling down the slope.

Folklore alleges that some people have domesticated the sidehill gouger, as it is useful for labor on steep terrain. One 1928 source purports that the species evolved from a strain of long-haired horses imported from Ireland. Despite this claim, most other sources maintain that the sidehill gouger is more deer-like than horse-like and is indigenous to North America. One variety from West Virginia lives on mountainsides so steep that the fur on one side of its body is completely rubbed off. The hide is polished, toughened, and naturally tanned, fetching a high price in the leather market. The other side of its body is covered with dense, shaggy wool.

STIFF-LEGGED BEAR

Many eastern Native American tribes describe a human-eating monster known variously as the stiff-legged bear, the naked bear, or Big Man-Eater. As its name suggests, the monster is usually perceived as a bear or is compared to one, although it is far larger than any ordinary bear. It has a disproportionately large head and is thus able to devour its human prey quickly. It also has oddly straight or stiff-jointed legs. Iroquoian-speaking tribes describe the creature as being naked or hairless. In some descriptions it has long teeth or tusks. The Creek and Seminole regard it as being more feline than bear-like and simply call it Man-Eater. Some tribes know it as Great Beast. Although the creature's description varies between cultures, the different versions are generally recognized as the same animal.

There is some debate as to whether the stiff-legged bear was actually a mastodon. This theory is fueled by the fact that some southeastern Native Americans reportedly said "Big Man-Eater" the first time they saw an African elephant at a zoo. Elephants share many qualities in common with the legendary monster; namely, their size, large head, stiff legs, and nearly impenetrable, naked skin. However, elephants and their kin are herbivores, and the possession of a trunk is not associated with the stiff-legged bear. It is unlikely that this mythical creature represents a case of residual memory of living Ice Age pachyderms, as some people have suggested. It is more likely that First Nations peoples were inspired to create the stiff-legged bear after discovering mammoth or mastodon bones in the ground.

TEEHOOLTSODII

Teehooltsodii, or Tééhoołtsódii, is a creature from Diné or Navajo mythology. This sacred beast presides over bodies of water and the direction of east. Its name means "Big Water Creature" or "Water Monster." It has epithets of One Who Grabs in Deep Water and Holy Being Who Controls the Waters. Teehooltsodii is described as an enormous otter with two horns, one black and one gold. In some versions it is female and in others it is male.

The Teehooltsodii appears in the Navajo creation story, where history is divided into different worlds. Present day is in the Fourth World, but the Teehooltsodii story takes place in the Third World. In this tale, the monster abducted two little girls swimming in the river and brought them to live with her own child. Search parties went out to find the missing children. First Man and First Woman eventually found them in the creature's lair and brought them home. The people rejoiced. Meanwhile, Coyote, the legendary trickster, picked up Teehooltsodii's baby.

Before long, all the animals were found running past the people in droves, heading toward a gigantic mountain. The people looked back and saw that the water was rapidly rising from the river and swallowing the land. They followed the animals and rushed to the top of the mountain. There they climbed through a hole in the sky and emerged into the Fourth World. The Third World became completely filled up with water. Teehooltsodii floated up and peered angrily into the Fourth World. Coyote gave her back her child and the water subsided. Teehooltsodii returned to the Third World, while the people and other animals remained in the Fourth.

THUNDERBIRD

The iconic mythical bird of North America occurs in many different forms across numerous indigenous tribes. Yet, all accounts agree that thunderbirds are generally eagle-like in their shape and are much larger than ordinary eagles. They are also known for their awe-inspiring power, being able to wield command over the elements of nature. Thunderbirds are said to produce thunder by flapping their wings and can throw lightning bolts from their claws. Usually they can only be seen by holy men, who can only see part of the bird at a time, due to the bird's tremendous sacred power.

The most famous thunderbirds come from the Lakota peoples of the Great Plains. Four great thunderbirds, named the Wakinyan Tanka, guard the four directions of the world. The one of the west is black, the one of the north is red, the one of the east is yellow, and the one of the south is white. The Wakinyans' job is to protect all that is sacred. These thunderbirds once fought a great battle against a pair of horned serpents called the Unktehi. Defeated, the Unktehis' bones became the great jagged rocks of the Badlands.

In many regions, thunderbirds are regarded as the enemies of horned serpents. Yet in the Pacific Northwest, giant serpents are seen as the thunderbolts that thunderbirds produce. According to the Ojibway, giant serpents are the thunderbirds' food. Among the Winnebago of Wisconsin, it is believed that thunderbirds also eat the flesh of people slain in battle. Thunderbirds in the Pacific Northwest prey on whales. Earthquakes are produced when a thunderbird drops a whale on the ground.

UGJUKNARPAK

According to the Netsilik Inuit, certain islands and areas of water may be inhabited by a dreadful beast called the ugjuknarpak. Whale hunters and other travelers are always warned to avoid passing through these particular stretches of water. The ugjuknarpak is shaped like a mouse but is enormous in size. It possesses a long, prehensile tail and hard skin that cannot be pierced by a harpoon. An upturned *umiak*, or whaling boat, is potentially a sign that the human-eating monster is present underneath. Yet, if someone comes across this sight, it may be too late to turn back.

One day a group of men embarked on their *umiak* to hunt for whales. Unfortunately, the whales had been last seen heading through a passage that was considered ugjuknarpak territory. Yet, their families were very hungry, so the lead hunter reluctantly decided it was worth the risk. The men rowed out through the forbidden channel. They spied the pod of whales in the distance, but before they could reach them, the water stirred.

An enormous rodent rose up, leering at them with hungry black eyes. The hunters hurled their harpoons at the ugjuknarpak, yet the weapons merely bounced off the monster's hide. Frantically they tried to row away. Suddenly their boat was seized by a great serpentine tail, which the beast had cast upon them like a lasso. It flipped the *umiak* over, dumping all the men into the freezing water. Then it lashed out again with its tail and snared each man one by one, drowning them. Nothing but their boat was left behind, floating upside down in the water.

UNDERWATER PANTHER

The underwater panther or Underwater Lynx is known to many First Nations in the eastern half of North America, spanning from subarctic Canada to the southern states. Its appearance varies between cultures. It is most commonly associated with the Ojibway, who call it Mishipeshu. This sacred being has the essence of a panther, yet it does not always look like one. In many depictions it has horns and a row of sharp spines down its back. It may even have a scaly body. Among some tribes it is allied with the horned serpent or is even conflated with this creature, as in the Iroquois version. As with the horned serpent, the underwater panther is often the enemy of the thunderbird, as its underwater domain is considered oppositional to the sky.

The underwater panther is associated with the violent aspects of water, such as rapids, whirlpools, floods, and large waves. The sound of rapids and waterfalls is the creature's roar. It uses its long, powerful tail to create disturbances in the water, sometimes overturning boats and drowning people who trespass into its realm. The underwater panther represents forces of nature that are dangerous, but not evil per se. Some tribes regard it as a guardian spirit of the water who may potentially extend its grace to protect humans. The underwater panther is generally respected for its power, and some tribes leave offerings for it. This being is also known as the guardian of copper ore. It is believed to have sunk many boats of those who came to Lake Superior to harvest copper without permission.

WAMPUS CAT

The wampus cat of the American Southeast is thought to have originated as a Cherokee mythical being called the Ewah. This creature was once a woman. Frequently, the woman's husband would go out at night and refuse to tell her what he was doing. One night she disguised herself by wearing a panther skin and spied on him from the bushes. She saw her husband meet with a group of men and perform a sacred hunting ritual. This ritual was forbidden to outsiders, especially women. The men discovered the eavesdropping wife and punished her with a curse. The panther skin magically fused to her body, transforming her into the Ewah, or wampus cat. Since then she is said to stalk the forests at night, looking for revenge.

The wampus cat persists in the contemporary folklore of the southeastern states. It has evolved away from its Cherokee origin yet maintains an overall reputation as a dangerous beast. In some regions its cry is said to be an omen of death. Despite its sinister reputation, the monstrous feline is part of the folk heritage of the Southeast, and some schools have embraced it as their mascot.

Interpretations of the cat's appearance vary. Some depict the wampus cat as an anthropomorphic panther like the original Ewah. Other times it is shaped like a normal panther with unusual coloration, such as black fur with a white rump. Some portrayals give the wampus cat six legs. It usually has glowing eyes and is larger than a normal panther. A seemingly unrelated wampus cat appears in Henry H. Tryon's 1939 comic bestiary, *Fearsome Critters*.

WENDIGO

Grotesque human-eating giants are one of the most ubiquitous classes of monster in First Nations folklore. The wendigo is a regional variant of this theme from the Algonquian-speaking tribes in northeastern North America. Some tribes refer to it as the chenoo. The monster's appearance varies by locality. In some versions it is tall, scrawny, and corpse-like, with gray skin and an odor of decay. In others it sports horns, large fangs, and glowing red eyes. Sometimes it is made out of ice. Occasionally it is said to be hairy like the Sasquatch. In all versions, it is a human who is transformed into a monster after committing a heinous act such as cannibalism or murder. It is also generally associated with ice, winter, and starvation. The monster's appetite for human flesh is never sated. In some regional variants it will grow larger with each meal, so that its stomach is never full.

Most mythical beings from First Nations belief systems are not pigeonholed as "good" or "evil." Yet, the wendigo is an exception: it is decidedly evil. It embodies the concept of moral corruption, especially gluttony and obsession. The myth of the wendigo serves to reinforce social taboos. Algonquian-speaking Native Americans traditionally believed that wendigoes can take a solid form as well as a spirit form. In spirit form, the monster can possess people and cause them to become cannibals. This phenomenon is referred to by Native people as "going wendigo," and by anthropologists as "wendigo psychosis." Supposedly this psychosis is a mental illness that actually existed, although there have not been any recent cases.

Chapter Two
LATIN AMERICA

Latin America consists of Mexico, Central America, South America, and the Caribbean Islands. These historically separate regions only became grouped together after being colonized by Spain and other "Latin" countries. Beginning around 1500 CE, Spaniards and other western Europeans violently conquered the indigenous peoples. Yet, the Americas were already home to several great empires. At various times, the Andes Mountains of South America harbored the Inca, Moche, Wari, Chimú, and Chavín civilizations. These were noteworthy for their ornate textiles, goldsmithing, unique terraced agriculture, stonemasonry, and medical knowledge. In Mesoamerica (Mexico and Central America), civilizations included the Aztecs, Mayas, Toltecs, Olmecs, and Teotihuacán. They are known for their architecture and advanced calendar. The Classic Maya of 300–850 CE also possessed ornate writing and a numeral system that was more advanced than Europe's at the time.

Contemporary Latin American folklore includes mythical creatures from Europe as well as ones from indigenous myth. This chapter focuses on the indigenous examples rather than the imports. Some Maya and Aztec monsters are included here, yet they do not compose the majority. The Guaraní of Paraguay and Mapuche of Chile and Argentina have myths full of monsters, and both contribute significantly to this chapter. Monster folklore thrives throughout Latin America, even today. Only a fraction of all their mythical creatures are included in this book. Many have never even been recorded in English.

AHUIZOTL

The ahuizotl ("ah-wee-sōtl") is a deadly water monster from Aztec mythology in central Mexico. This peculiar species resembles a dog in size and shape and is sometimes also compared to an otter, opossum, or monkey. It has human-like hands on all four limbs and an additional hand on the end of its long tail. It is either slick haired or hairless. The ahuizotl is associated with Tlaloc, the god of storms and water. All persons sacrificed to Tlaloc, as well as anyone who dies a water-related death, have the privilege of spending eternity in an underwater paradise called Tlalocán. Yet, perhaps all these deaths are not enough for Tlaloc, as the ahuizotl claims additional victims for the god.

Ahuizotls are known to stalk the waters surrounding the underwater caves in which they make their lairs. They seize fishermen and other unfortunate passersby at any opportunity, using their specialized tail to choke the victims and drag them underwater. If an ahuizotl has not been able to capture any human prey in a long time, it will resort to crying like a child. It will then seize any person who seeks out the source of the crying. The predator's favorite food is human eyeballs, teeth, and fingernails. Others say it keeps these parts as trophies. After killing its victim, it releases their body to the surface, which is intact minus the aforementioned parts. All of its victims were considered sacrifices to Tlaloc and therefore died with honor. Only priests were allowed to remove their bodies from the water due to the holiness of the circumstances.

ALICANTO

One of Chile's numerous mythical species, the alicanto is a bird that subsists on gold and silver. It originated among the Mapuche yet today is considered generically Chilean. There are numerous interpretations of the alicanto across different regions. All versions agree that the bird emits light the color of the metal that it consumes, either silver or gold. According to some, there are even alicantos that feed on copper and glow green. It is a flightless bird, yet it is capable of running quickly. It is said to lay eggs with gold or silver shells, and its feathers are also metallic. The bird's size is less widely agreed upon. Some older sources describe it as being very large, perhaps even predatory, with dangerous claws. Other descriptions suggest it is smaller and more harmless.

The alicanto is primarily associated with the Atacama Desert, spanning through northern Chile. It may inhabit caves, mines, or forests. Its presence, detectable by a light seen at night, indicates deposits of precious ore nearby. It is commonly thought that the alicanto's inability to fly is due to the weight of the metal in its belly. Treasure hunters often attempt to pursue this bird in hopes that it will lead them to its food source. However, these birds are usually aware of being followed and are infamous for luring people off cliffs to their death. Others say it is good luck to see an alicanto or be shone upon by its light. Some claim an alicanto may occasionally favor a lucky person and willingly share its silver or gold with them.

AO AO

Ao Ao is one of seven monsters of Guaraní mythology, coming from Paraguay and neighboring countries. Ao Ao and his brothers came into being when Tau, the spirit of evil, abducted and married a woman named Kerana, long ago. The moon goddess Arasy punished Tau with a curse, and thus all his sons were born as mutants and monsters. Ao Ao was the sixth of the seven and is the deadliest of the lot.

The description of his appearance differs regionally. In ancient times he was most certainly compared to a wild pig-like animal called a peccary. In postcolonial times he is described as either pig-like or sheep-like, or a cross between the two. Occasionally he is said to look like a sheep with a wolf's head. In all cases, he has long fangs and claws instead of hooves.

Ao Ao is extremely fertile and prolific, having generated many others of his own kind. Due to his reproductive prowess, he is regarded as an archetype of fertility. He is also the ruler of the hills and mountains. Yet, despite looking like a sheep, Ao Ao is a bloodthirsty predator. Humans are his favorite prey. His name comes from the cry that he makes as he pursues his quarry, "*Ao, ao, ao!*" If a person is being pursued by an Ao Ao, it will chase them until they collapse from exhaustion, or until they climb to the top of a palm tree. Palm trees are sacred in Guaraní beliefs, and Ao Ao cannot knock them down. If it is any other tree, however, he will dig at the roots and ram the tree with his head until it falls.

CAMAZOTZ

Camazotz is a type of gigantic monster bat from Maya mythology. Its name means "sudden-attack bat." This species appears in the *Popol Vuh*, the sacred text of the Highland Mayas in Guatemala. Camazotz bats have long, protruding fangs, like the blades of knives, that jut forward from their faces. These creatures are depicted in Mayan and Zapotec art as anthropomorphic, standing upright like a person rather than hanging upside down like normal bats. Their wings are decorated with gruesome ornaments such as human bones and gouged-out eyeballs.

Reputed to be able to eat the moon, the Camazotz bats are fearsome beasts sent forth by the gods to dispatch unrighteous mortals. Camazotz bats dwell in Xibalba, the land of the dead. They inhabit a dungeon known as Bat House. This is one of several houses of challenge used by the lords of Xibalba to dispose of living people who trespass in the land of the dead.

One day, the Xibalba lords decided they had enough of the Hero Twins, Hunahpú and Xbalanqué, who played ball games loudly on the court directly above. They called the Hero Twins down to Xibalba to have them killed. The twins were forced to stay overnight in the various houses of challenge. The brothers cleverly eluded defeat each time until they spent the night in Bat House. Xbalanqué successfully hid from the giant bats, yet Hunahpú had his head snatched off by a Camazotz. The creature then brought the head to the two Xibalba lords. Xbalanqué eventually won his brother's head back by beating the Xibalba lords in a ball game.

CHONCHÓN

The chonchón is an infamous type of *wekufe* from Mapuche folklore in Chile and Argentina. Witches often summon evil spirits called wekufes and send them to do their bidding. The horrible chonchón is one of the witches' favorite standbys. There are many regional variants of the chonchón, as there are many different groups among the Mapuche people. They generally regard it as a type of bird, although it is actually understood to be a flying human head. Some Mapuches claim the chonchón is a witch who has transformed herself, and the head is her own head. Others believe witches can produce chonchóns by cutting off the head of a dead person and magically bringing it to life. The head may transform into the shape of a bird, or a bird with the head of a person. Other times it may literally look like a human head that flies around on its own, its ears having turned into wings, and with talons where its neck should be.

The chonchón is one of several wekufes that spreads disease and misfortune by sucking out people's blood. Chonchóns strike at night, especially on moonless nights. They are almost always invisible. The chonchón can attack its victims without their knowing it, and the person will fall ill for no apparent reason. A person who is already ill is especially vulnerable to further assault by the creature. Although the chonchón is rarely seen, many Mapuches believe they have heard its chilling cry. They believe that if someone hears it calling out above their house at night, a resident of the house will soon die.

CHUPACABRAS

The chupacabras, chupacabra, or goatsucker has become very famous in recent times. It is not an indigenous myth, yet neither is it a European import. The cryptid monster recognized today was born in Puerto Rico in 1995. Sightings quickly spread to Mexico and other Latin American countries, and even to the United States. The initial description of the creature resembled the popular North American conception of an extraterrestrial alien, yet with added bestial features. These features include a row of spines down its back, large red eyes, sharp teeth, small arms, and powerful hind legs like a kangaroo's. From one report cascaded hundreds of other sightings with wildly varying descriptions. Sometimes the creature was said to be more humanoid, sometimes more reptilian, and sometimes winged. In the US, it came to be identified with diseased coyotes. As a goatsucker, the chupacabras is believed to kill livestock by drinking the animal's blood.

North Americans speculated that the chupacabras was a pet left behind by alien visitors. But Latin Americans circulated more-sinister theories. They supposed that the chupacabras was created by the United States, either as a scientific experiment or accidentally through chemical pollution. These fears reflected sociopolitical tensions between the US and Puerto Rico. Yet, the most likely origin of the chupacabras is mass hysteria. The very first sketch of a spiny, alien-like monster was published in a newspaper following a report by one woman. This woman later admitted to having watched the Hollywood science fiction thriller, *Species*, a few weeks prior. Her monster looked remarkably similar to a fictional alien that appeared in that movie.

CUERO

The name *cuero* is Spanish for cowhide. This strange aquatic creature resembles a large animal hide that has been stretched out. It is a generic class of water monster in Chile and Patagonia. It is sometimes described as flat and circular in shape, with claws along its edges. In some localities, the cuero has a distinct head, while in others it is more shapeless. It has eyes that may bulge out or are on the ends of stalks, or there may be many of them around the perimeter of its body. On its underside it has tentacles and a mouth. Although it has a Spanish name, this South American monster is of indigenous origin and is thought to predate colonization. The Mapuche peoples of Chile and Argentina call it Trelquehuecuve, meaning "evil hide creature."

Cueros can dwell in fresh or salt water, but they are most frequently encountered in small, dark lakes. Lago Lácar in western Argentina is infamously noted to harbor one or more of these monsters. Cueros sometimes float to the surface of the water, imitating harmless animal hides dropped by humans. They are also known to drag themselves up onto the bank and sun themselves on rocks. If a person or animal walks over a cuero, or touches one in the water, the creature will suddenly envelop them and suffocate them. It feeds on the blood of its victims using its sucker-like mouth. The Mapuches know to kill a cuero by throwing a thorny cactus at it. The creature will instinctively wrap around the cactus and die of puncture wounds. Cueros may have been inspired by stingrays.

CUYANCÚA

El Salvador harbors its own unique mythical creature known as the cuyancúa, the half pig, half snake. It has the head and forelimbs of a wild pig, bearing tusks, and the rest of its body is a serpent's. Statues of the creature can be found at the Atecozol Resort in Sonsonate, a popular tourist site. These statues further embellish the creature with a small horn on its head. Folklore surrounding the cuyancúa is associated with the western part of the country, and especially with the locality of Izalco. This region is famous for its numerous stories about magic and the supernatural. Belief in the cuyancúa originated long ago among the indigenous people of the area, known as the Pipils or Cuzcatlecs.

Individuals who claim to have seen the cuyancúa report being so overcome with terror that they faint. The creature produces a blood-chilling scream that can sometimes be heard at night. It can also create a loud noise by raising the bristles on its back and vibrating them together. It is unclear whether or not this animal actually harms people. The idea that the cuyancúa is evil is most likely a Christian reinterpretation of an earlier legend. In ancient times, the Pipils believed the cuyancúa was a guardian of water and a spirit of rain. It was able to control the rain and produce fresh, drinkable water from the earth. It would have been half peccary rather than half pig, as the true pig was imported by the Spaniards. After the native people were converted to Catholicism, the nature spirits they formerly revered were recast as evil ghosts and demons.

FEATHERED SERPENT

The iconic feathered serpent, or plumed serpent, is probably the most widely known mythical creature from any indigenous people of Latin America. This great magical serpent is covered with the green feathers of a bird called the quetzal. North Americans sometimes inaccurately depict the creature with wings and incorrectly attribute it to South America. In actuality it has no wings but is nonetheless able to fly. It comes from Mexico, not South America. The mystical serpents are believed to hold various symbolic associations with the sky, water, and fertility.

The oldest known image of a feathered serpent appears on an Olmec bas relief called Monument 19, from La Venta. The date of this monument is unknown, but it may be over 3,000 years old. Since then, feathered serpents have appeared in the artwork of other civilizations, including the Aztecs, Mayas, Toltecs, and Teotihuacán. One of the most famous monuments depicting feathered serpents is the Temple of the Sun at the Toltec-Maya site of Chichén Itzá. A statue of the creature's stylized head is placed on a pedestal on either side of the pyramid staircase. During the solstices, the multilayered pyramid casts an undulating shadow that lines up with the heads, forming the serpent's body.

Many sources refer to the feathered serpent by its Nahuatl or Aztec name, Quetzalcoatl ("ket-sal-KO-ahtl"). This name literally means "feathered snake," although it can also mean "precious twin." Quetzalcoatl is also the name of a prominent deity in the Aztec pantheon, who is the god of wind and creator of civilization. Normally human shaped, he has the ability to transform into a feathered serpent at will.

GURUVILU

The guruvilu is a dangerous aquatic beast from South America. Its name means fox snake in Mapudungun, the Mapuche language. Specifically, the word *guru* refers to a female fox. Regional variants of its name in different dialects include glyryvilu, nguruvilu, and nirivilo. The creature has a fox's head, an elongated body, and a long tail with a claw at the end. Sometimes it is interpreted as a more feline animal, despite its name. This "fox snake" is considered to be a generic class of water monster by the indigenous peoples of Chile and Argentina. As such, it is sometimes confused with the region's other generic class of water monster, the cuero. Although they do not look anything alike, both classes of monsters will drag a person underwater and eat them.

The Mapuches warn that the guruvilu will kill any person who attempts to wade or swim across a body of water that it inhabits. They often say that it drowns its victims by snagging them with its tail claw and pulling them underwater. Alternatively, it may stretch out its long body and constrict them like a snake. The only potentially safe way to cross the water is by boat. However, even this is not guaranteed, as the guruvilu is known to occasionally overturn canoes with its tail. It is also capable of creating whirlpools.

The only person who can defeat a guruvilu is a shaman called a *machi*. Traditionally, most machis were women. A machi can wade into the water and threaten the beast with a knife, demanding that it stops attacking people. The creature must submit due to the machi's magical powers.

HUALLEPÉN

The huallepén, or waillepén, is a *wekufe* from Mapuche folklore in Chile and Argentina. It appears as a gnarled, deformed, hairless sheep or llama with the head of a calf. Its name means "sheep calf." The different wekufes, or evil spirits, are believed to be responsible for various maladies and misfortunes. The huallepén's niche is in causing birth defects, particularly in livestock. For the past 200 years, the Mapuche economy has depended heavily on herding cattle and sheep. Prior to this, the Mapuche herded llamas, as cattle and sheep were imported later by the Spaniards. Therefore, the huallepén may have originally been based on a llama instead of a sheep or bovine calf. Today this creature is one of the most infamous wekufes.

The huallepén prefers to spend most of its time in water. It cannot walk on land, as its legs are utterly twisted and malformed, mimicking a common birth defect among sheep and cattle. The huallepén is so misshapen that it must crawl or hop like a seal. In some interpretations it actually has the hindquarters of a seal instead of legs. The creature is seldom seen, yet people sometimes hear its terrible cry. At night the huallepén is said to come out of the water to mate with cows and sheep. It impregnates them with offspring that have twisted legs, facial deformities, or other defects. Worst of all, its evil power can affect humans in a similar manner. If sighted by a pregnant woman, it can cause deformities in the unborn baby. It can also spread its curse by haunting women in their dreams.

LUISÓN

Luisón is the youngest of the seven sons of Tau in Guaraní mythology. Despite colonization, the myth of this ghastly monster remains prevalent in Paraguay and surrounding countries. This may be due in part to the popular Latin American tradition of telling ghost stories, to which Luisón easily adapts. Luisón has been reinterpreted from the original myth and thus has changed much over the centuries. In modern folklore, he embodies the principle of death, not unlike the Grim Reaper. His dominion is the graveyard. It is said that a person in a graveyard at midnight might feel a cold, clammy hand on their shoulder and hear Luisón whisper to them that death is nigh. A person who experiences this can break the curse if they invoke Luisón's name three times over the soil in their garden. They must then place a bit of the soil under their tongue.

Luisón is traditionally described as a grotesque, bestial humanoid who walks on all fours. His hair is long and black, draping down over much of his body. His skin is ghastly white. He has fangs and other characteristics of an animal. Contemporary South

Americans regard Luisón as a werewolf, yet wolves were unknown in the Guaraní region in precolonial times. The werewolf myth is a European import. Prior to colonization, he may have been perceived as more feline than canine. His original Guaraní name was Huiso. The modern name, Luisón, probably arose by combining Huiso with lobizon, the word for werewolf used in Argentina. The Guaraní today accept the monster's name change and readily describe him as *hombre lobo*, or "wolf man."

MAPINGUARÍ

The mapinguarí is a popular folk monster from Brazil. It is not attributed to any one specific tribe but is associated generally with the western Amazon. It is most likely the product of combining stories from various cultures. There are many regional variants of the mapinguarí, yet it is always a large humanoid covered with shaggy hair. It has one large eye in the middle of its face, and in many descriptions, its cavernous mouth is located on its torso. The creature is generally described as having long, powerful arms and short, stubby legs. As with many mythical forest-dwelling beings, the mapinguarí is often said to have backward-pointing feet, or no feet at all. It also smells horrendous.

Many rural Brazilians believe in the mapinguarí's existence. Although seldom seen, it is known for its eerie, piercing cry. The creature is sometimes regarded as a protector of the forest, as it is reputed to attack hunters and loggers. It is also a carnivore that will include humans in its diet. The mapinguarí is notoriously difficult to kill, as it has thick skin-like an alligator beneath its fur. According to some, the only ways to kill this monster are by stabbing it in the navel or by setting it on fire.

There is presumably more than one mapinguarí. It is sometimes said that these creatures are former humans. Some indigenous people believe that if an old man abandons his tribe to live alone in the forest, he will transform into a mapinguarí. Some cryptozoology enthusiasts have suggested that the mapinguarí may be a giant ground sloth.

MBÓI TU'I

Mbói Tu'i is a monster from Guaraní mythology in Paraguay and neighboring countries. There are many waterways in the jungle where the Guaraní live, and these waters are said to be protected by Mbói Tu'i. The creature's name means "parrot snake," as he is an enormous serpent with the head of a parrot. Sometimes he is also described as having two small limbs like a lizard's front legs. According to legend, Mbói Tu'i was killed in a fire long ago, along with his brothers. Nonetheless, the Guaraní often speak of Mbói Tu'i as though he is still alive in the tributaries of the Amazon River. He is an archetypal spirit who presides over the wetlands, aquatic creatures, flowers, and dew. He is seldom seen, yet some say they have heard his blood-chilling squawk echoing through the trees.

Mbói Tu'i was born as the result of a curse from the Guaraní moon goddess, Arasy. Long ago, an evil spirit named Tau abducted a woman named Kerana. Angatupry, the spirit of good, tried to stop Tau but was not successful. Furious, the moon goddess punished him by causing all of his children to be monsters and mutants. Mbói Tu'i was the second of these children. Although terrible in appearance, he is one of the more innocuous among them. He keeps to himself in the rivers and swamps, rarely causing trouble for anyone. Even still, Mbói Tu'i is an accursed offspring of the spirit of evil. He is potentially dangerous if provoked. The Guaraní regard him conflictingly both as a sacred nature spirit and an abomination.

MOÑAI

Moñai is an infamous villain from Guaraní mythology. Some artistic renderings depict him as a ghoulish humanoid, yet oftentimes he is described as an enormous serpent with large teeth and two horns. These horns are long and straight and brightly colored. They generate a magical power with which Moñai can hypnotize his prey, which usually consists of birds. He presides over the domain of countryside and open spaces. He also rules the air and may be able to fly, although he does not have wings.

Moñai is the third of the seven sons of Tau, and a notorious thief. According to the myth, the seven monstrous brothers plagued the Guaraní for years. Moñai, with his rampant thievery, was the most troublesome. His stealthy crimes caused people to point fingers at one another for their stolen goods and damaged property. Before long, their society degenerated into violent chaos.

Finally, a man named Tume Arandu, and his sister, Porasy, came to destroy Moñai and his brothers. Porasy seduced Moñai and asked him to marry her. Moñai had never had a human visitor and was so stunned by this maiden's beauty that he said yes. Porasy required that Moñai and all of his brothers come together and meet her family before the wedding. The monsters then congregated inside a cave and held a party, drinking *chicha* and becoming intoxicated. Tume waited outside the cave and sealed the entrance. He set fire to a great pile of wood, eventually killing everyone inside. Porasy has been immortalized in song for her self-sacrifice. Her spirit became the morning star, and the monsters became constellations in the night sky.

MUQUI

The Andes Mountains of South America harbor numerous mines for coal, iron, gold, and other minerals. The muqui ("MOO-kee") is a goblin-like being said to inhabit these mines in Peru, Bolivia, Ecuador, and Colombia. This creature is similar to the gnomes and elves of European folklore, which may lead one to assume he was introduced by the Spaniards. In actuality, the muqui originated as an indigenous mountain spirit. This being is typically imagined as a little man about 2–3 feet tall, often red skinned, with light blond hair. He is frequently depicted with two horns on his head. His clothing varies but often consists of mining gear. He may carry a lantern or a flashlight. He can also shapeshift into animals or a white man. In some regions the muqui is a race or class of beings. Alternative names are anchancho and Supay.

Christianity was quick to demonize indigenous beliefs and equate the muqui with the devil. Some people in mining communities are now afraid of him, thinking him to be evil. The negative association with this being has also been merged with the social stigmas attached to laboring in the mines. Some miners identify the muqui with silicon dioxide, which is toxic to inhale. Yet, prior to the introduction of Christianity, the muqui was believed to be a steward of the land. Many believe the muqui is merely mischievous, not actually evil. Some believe he is actually harmless or even friendly. In Bolivia, some miners place clay effigies of the protective underground spirit in the mine as they work. They often refer to him as El Tío, or "uncle."

PIHUICHEN

The pihuichen, also spelled piwichen, is one of the *wekufes*, or evil supernatural beings feared by the Mapuche and Puelche peoples of Chile and Argentina. This sinister creature is said to look like a snake with the leathery wings of a bat. This flying snake is not necessarily large, yet it is extremely dangerous. One does not even need to be bitten by this serpent in order to die. Merely looking at it can be deadly. There are many different regional variants of this myth. Oftentimes it is said to be a shapeshifter. In some accounts it is believed to undergo a metamorphosis over the course of its life and may turn into a bird.

When one person sees a pihuichen approaching, everyone turns and runs, hides, or even flops face down on the ground to avoid being affected by its evil magic. The terrible creature produces a whistling cry, "*Piurit, piurit!*" This causes people to look at it, thus afflicting them with its curse. Many Mapuches also believe the pihuichen will suck the blood out of people and livestock. This behavior is commonplace among wekufes and is a way of explaining the occurrence of disease. Yet, a pihuichen may not merely leave its victims ill as other wekufes do. It is said to suck out every last drop of blood until the victim's body is completely dry. Its name means "to dry a person." It sometimes attacks humans but more frequently attacks cattle. Any livestock animal found inexplicably dead is presumed to have been killed by the pihuichen.

QUETZALCOATL

—See *Feathered Serpent*.

TEJU JAGUA

T eju Jagua is one of the accursed offspring of Tau in Guaraní mythology. He was
the first of the seven sons and the most monstrous. According to some descriptions,
he has seven dog heads and the body of an enormous lizard. Others say he has only
one head instead of seven, but it is seven times the size of a normal head. He also has
flames flashing from his eyes. Teju Jagua's head or heads are so heavy that he cannot
walk. He is therefore confined to a cave known as Yaguarón. Since he cannot exit the
cave, he is brought food by his brother, Jasy Jateré. The least grotesque of the brothers,
Jasy Jateré looks like an androgynous human child with long, golden hair.

Teju Jagua was such a horror upon birth that Tupa, the creator god, intervened.
Tupa prevented his ferocity from developing as he matured. Teju Jagua is therefore

not only immobile, but gentle by nature and essentially harmless. In some regional variants of the myth, Teju Jagua is still inherently vicious, yet Tupa confined him to a cave and mired him down in mud and water to prevent him from destroying the world. In yet another variant, Teju Jagua is docile because of his sweet diet of fruit and honey. Nonetheless, his appearance is enough to instill terror in the hearts of the bravest warriors. Teju Jagua is known as the lord of caves and the guardian of hidden treasure. In the official myth, he was killed in a fire. Yet some Guaraní say he is still alive somewhere underground.

TLALTECUHTLI

Also known simply as the Earth Monster, Tlaltecuhtli ("tlal-teh-COOT-lee") was the primordial beast whose body became the land in Aztec mythology. This enormous creature is often depicted in humanoid form. It had many eyes, many noses, and many mouths, in various parts of its body. Its skin was like an alligator's. Sometimes Tlaltecuhtli is depicted as a colossal reptile or a humanoid with an alligator head and claws. The gender of this being is uncertain. The name Tlaltecuhtli means "Earth Lord" and is masculine, yet it is sometimes depicted as a female squatting in birth-giving position.

Tlaltecuhtli existed in a primordial sea near the abode of the gods. The god Tezcatlipoca had stepped into the sea, when Tlaltecuhtli immediately closed its jaws and bit off his foot. Tezcatlipoca then summoned his brother, Quetzalcoatl, and the two gods grappled with Tlaltecuhtli. Tezcatlipoca and Quetzalcoatl each grabbed one of the monster's arms, and one of its legs and tore the creature in half. Half of its body became the earth and half became the sky.

Yet, despite being torn apart, Tlaltecuhtli was not dead. It cried out loudly with pain and anger. Its many jaws snapped open and shut and its body quaked. The other gods descended and transformed its eyes into lakes and ponds, its noses into mountains, and its mouths into chasms and caverns. They made trees and vegetation grow from its flesh. But still, Tlaltecuhtli cried out. The only thing that would satisfy it was blood. Tlaltecuhtli continues to quake and cry for blood to this day. This is one of the explanations given as to why the Aztecs practiced human sacrifice.

VUCUB CAQUIX

The Highland Maya epic, the *Popol Vuh*, describes a mythical character named Vucub Caquix ("voo-KOOB ka-KEESH"). His name means Seven Macaw. It was common for Mayan names to include numbers, as these numbers held astronomical significance. Vucub Caquix resembled his namesake bird, the scarlet macaw, yet he also had human-like characteristics such as teeth. In Lowland sources he is often imagined as a gigantic macaw, while in the Highlands he is portrayed as more humanoid. He had two sons who were giants and were not bird-like. Yet Vucub Caquix behaved like a bird, as he would perch in trees and refer to his home as a nest. Presumably he was able to fly. The Maya also identify him with the Big Dipper constellation.

Vucub Caquix was a truly spectacular being. He lived during a time when the land was populated by spirits and demigods, while modern humans did not yet exist. The sun and moon were concealed behind clouds. Instead, Vucub Caquix was the world's source of light. He was radiant and powerful, brilliantly colored, with large shining teeth, and jewels and precious metals growing on his face and body. He brashly denigrated the creator god and proclaimed his own dominion over the world. The Hero Twins, Hunahpú and Xbalanqué, decided that Vucub Caquix must be eliminated before the world would be safe for mortal humans. One day, the twins hid behind his favorite tree, and when Vucub Caquix descended into it, they shot him in the jaw with a blowgun. This caused him to lose his teeth, which were the source of his power. He then quickly faded and died.

WATER TIGER

Water tigers are a class of mysterious predator described in many parts of South America. Despite the recurrent nature of these cryptids, there is considerable variation in their description regionally. For this reason, they are probably not an existing species, despite being zoologically plausible. One variant comes from the Shuar natives of Ecuador, who live in the Cloud Forest of the Andes. They refer to the water tiger as entzaeia-yawá. It has webbed feet like an otter but is specified to be a feline. It has long hair on its tail and possibly all over its body. It is thought to live in the water full-time, rather than merely hunting in it. The Shuar sometimes blame this dangerous predator when people go missing near the river.

The Tehuelche people of Patagonia describe a beast called the iemisch, also called the water tiger. It resembles a giant otter but has large fangs and claws and possesses an impenetrable hide. In 1774, the English Jesuit priest Thomas Falkner was warned of another water tiger, the yaguaru. This purportedly looks like a giant otter with the head of a wolf and saber teeth. Many fishermen and farmers along the Amazon River fear attack by another beast called the onça d'água, or water jaguar. This is said to have unusually long, droopy ears, which create a distinctive noise when slapping against the water as it swims. It is also noted for its vile odor, which can cause people to fall ill. While many rural Brazilians believe this creature exists in flesh and blood, some of them also believe it is a supernatural entity from the spirit world.

WERE-JAGUAR

Were-jaguar is a term used by archeologists, referring to any being with a combination of human and jaguar features. This term is primarily associated with imagery from the Olmec civilization of ancient Mexico, which lasted from approximately 1500 to 400 BCE. Archeologists have unearthed numerous were-jaguar figurines from Olmec sites, often made out of jade. The were-jaguars vary in appearance, some having more-feline features than others. Many of them are fully human except for a snarling mouth with jaguar fangs. Similar-looking creatures have also been discovered in ancient Peruvian art and are known elsewhere in indigenous Latin American myth. These different regional motifs may not be related to each other, but they indicate that people in different places were in awe of the majestic jaguar.

The meaning of the were-jaguar is shrouded in mystery. One common assumption is that it was a figure of worship. Many indigenous cultures revere jaguars and consider them to be ancestral totems. An alternative hypothesis is that the were-jaguar figurines represent shapeshifters. Many indigenous peoples of Latin America, even today, believe that shamans have the ability to shapeshift into animals, especially jaguars. In some cultures, shamans use hallucinogens such as ayahuasca in their transformation process. In the Yucatec language of the Mayas, *balaam* is a word meaning both jaguar and sorcerer. Throughout Mexico, jaguars are associated with the concept of *nagual*, the animal spirit-double of a shaman. Nagual shapeshifting is a sacred spiritual power and not a curse, unlike in Christian European folklore of the werewolf. Nonetheless, after Christianity was introduced, nagual magic has become associated with evil sorcery and witchcraft.

XIUHCOATL

The name *xiuhcoatl* ("shee-OO-ko-ahtl") means "turquoise serpent" in Nahuatl, the language of the Aztecs. It is also known as the fire serpent, or *serpiente de fuego*, in English and Spanish. The Aztecs symbolically associated turquoise with fire, and the same word also meant year. The xiuhcoatl's tail ends in a sharp point identical to the ideogram for the word "year." The creature possesses large fangs like a viper yet otherwise bears only a vague resemblance to a snake. It has an elongated, recurved snout that curls upward above its face. It is also usually depicted with two front limbs, and occasionally four limbs, like an alligator. Sometimes it is portrayed with a segmented body and an upcurled tail, like a scorpion.

The xiuhcoatl appears in various codices and monuments and is even found in earlier Toltec art. It is considered a sacred being. The xiuhcoatl is the spirit animal or shapeshifted form of Xiuhtecuhtli, the Aztec god of fire. Xiuhtecuhtli is a warrior and ruler, a younger version of the elderly fire god, Huehueteotl. He is also associated with turquoise, daylight, the new year, and new life after death.

Yet the xiuhcoatl is more than simply an alternative shape of Xiuhtecuhtli. There was more than one of this creature. Sometimes two or four of them are depicted alongside one another. Huitzilopochtli, the god of war and the sun, wields a xiuhcoatl as a weapon. He used it to slay his enemy sister, the moon goddess Coyolxauhqui. The xiuhcoatl is associated with human sacrifice. In modern day, the Mexican military uses an assault rifle named the FX-05 Xiuhcoatl, in honor of their heritage.

ZIPACNÁ

The Maya mythical villain Vucub Caquix had two sons, who were giants named Zipacná and Cabrakán. At least one of these giants was reptilian: Zipacná, whose name means caiman or alligator. He is portrayed varyingly as an enormous alligator or as humanoid and may be a shapeshifter. He and his family were demigods who lived on the earth during a time before the gods created humans. Zipacná's role was to build the mountains. Yet he was also arrogant like his father, and he boasted that he created the earth itself. His moral character was ambiguous, as he was capable of both good and evil. He is commonly regarded as a villain.

Zipacná gained notoriety after his interactions with a group of young demigods (or perhaps protohumans) known as the Four Hundred Boys. At first he was amenable toward them, yet the Four Hundred Boys became fearful of his great strength. They devised a plot to kill him and then trapped him in a pit. Zipacná dug his way out of the pit, rose up, and crushed all the boys like insects.

After Zipacná committed this deed, the Hero Twins, Hunahpú and Xbalanqué, decided that they must eliminate him. The Hero Twins lured the alligator giant into a crevice at the base of a mountain. They created an artificial crab and planted it as bait. With their powers of illusion, they brought the crab to life and sent it scuttling deep into the crevice. Excited and predatory, Zipacná crawled in after the crab as far as he could go. Once he was so firmly wedged that he could no longer move, he turned into stone.

Chapter Three

ANCIENT GREECE AND ROME

Much of Western civilization traces its roots back to ancient Greek and Roman culture. Highly literate, these peoples generated voluminous myths, historical accounts, philosophical writings, plays, and other works that survive into modern day. Greece produced some of Europe's earliest philosophers, poets, architects, mathematicians, and other great minds. The Greeks even used one of the world's first alphabets, while the Roman alphabet became the standard writing system used around the world today. In the fourth century BCE, Alexander the Great conquered numerous kingdoms in the Balkan region, Anatolia, Egypt, and the Middle East. Later, the Roman Empire would come to engulf many of the same lands, as well as spreading westward throughout Europe. So definitive were Greece and Rome to Western history that Westerners refer to them as composing "Classical Civilization."

Due to their impact on European history, and their extensive mythological writings, the Greeks and Romans have set the basis of what most Westerners think of when they hear the word "mythology." These civilizations were exceptional when it comes to mythical creatures in particular. The ancient Greeks loved to create fearsome, fantastical monsters to accompany the gods and heroes of their complex myths. The Romans shared much of this same mythology. The distinctive legendary creatures of these ancient cultures have persisted in world literature forever since.

BASILISK

The horrific basilisk is a small creature known for its extreme deadliness. This serpent is so venomous that it can kill with its breath or its gaze, without ever having to touch its victims. Pliny the Elder wrote that its breath destroys all vegetation and can even split rocks. The basilisk's appearance is distinguished by a crest or crown on its head. This crown is the basis of its name, meaning "little king" in Greek. Eventually it came to be depicted as having a rooster's head and in medieval times took on a myriad of other forms. In some images the basilisk has up to eight legs. In others it has two legs and wings. In Christian Europe it evolved into the cockatrice, which resembles a rooster with a serpent's tail.

According to Lucan's *Pharsalia*, the basilisk was spawned from the blood of Medusa, which dripped out of the gorgon's severed head as Perseus carried it across the Libyan Desert. Lucan wrote that a Roman soldier named Murrus attempted to kill a basilisk with his spear. Instantly, the poison of the terrible creature spread through his spear and into his hand. It would have spread through his entire body and killed him, yet he quickly cut off his own arm to save his life. A story told in the Middle Ages claims that a basilisk killed a large number of Alexander the Great's troops as they prepared to besiege a foreign city. Alexander finally vanquished the creature by showing it its own reflection in a mirror. Other sources state that basilisks can be killed by weasels, roosters, and the herb rue.

CATOBLEPAS

The catoblepas is another deadly creature reputed to inhabit the African desert. It is known primarily from Roman bestiaries, although its name is Greek, meaning "downward looking." The Romans believed it lives in Ethiopia near the Nigris River. Classical descriptions of the catoblepas are vague. Only two things about it are consistent: it has a large, heavy head, which it rarely raises, and if it does lift its head, its gaze will kill anyone it sees.

The earliest known account comes from Pomponius Mela, writing around 44 CE. He wrote that the catoblepas is "of no great size," and while its gaze is deadly, it cannot harm anyone by biting or stinging. Pliny the Elder described it as creature of "moderate size" and inactive. Solinus called it "little" and "sluggish." None of them provided any details of its appearance. Claudius Aelianus, a contemporary of Solinus, was the first to compare the catoblepas to a bull in size and shape. He wrote that it has a mane like a horse that covers its eyes until it becomes startled. Yet, according to him, it is not the gaze of the creature that kills, but its breath, which is toxic from the poisonous roots it eats.

The catoblepas persisted throughout medieval and Renaissance times. Its appearance as a bovine animal became widely accepted, although writers disagreed on whether it kills with its eyes or its breath. The Late Renaissance scholar Edward Topsell added large dragon-like scales to the creature's description. He called it a Gorgon, although he maintained that it kills with its breath rather than its gaze. Later descriptions also gave it a pig-like head.

CENTAUR

The centaurs are among the oldest, most recognizable, and most enduring mythological creatures in the world. They are thought to have originated in the Bronze Age, predating classical Greek civilization. This time period coincides with the first domesticated horses being brought to Europe from central Eurasia. In early Greek mythology, all centaurs were male and were presumed to be immortal. Artists began depicting female centaurs later, calling them centaurides.

The centaurs were generally portrayed as people who have poor control over their baser natures. One especially infamous incident took place at the wedding feast of King Pirithous of the Lapiths. The centaur guests had no tolerance for alcohol and turned to rude behavior the moment they started drinking. They began overturning the dining tables and tried to abduct the women. One, named Eurytion, tried to take the bride. A violent battle ensued that was called the Centauromachy.

The most famous centaur was an exceptionally civilized individual named Chiron. Known for his wisdom and compassion, he served as a mentor to several Greek heroes,

including Achilles, Jason, Theseus, and Asclepius. Hercules had befriended Chiron as well as another civilized centaur named Pholus. While having dinner with the two of them, Hercules opened a bottle of wine. This attracted a horde of wild centaurs who were already intoxicated by the scent. Hercules fought them off with poisoned arrows, but he accidentally killed the two civilized centaurs in the process. According to some versions, this finished off the entire race. Chiron became immortalized as a constellation called Centaurus. He also later became associated with the zodiac sign Sagittarius.

CERBERUS

The underworld of Greek mythology is guarded by Cerberus, the monstrous three-headed dog. Ancient Greeks believed all mortal souls go to the realm of Hades after death. Hades is a dark world underground, although it is not a place of punishment. Cerberus is often depicted alongside the god of the underworld, who is called Hades by the Greeks and Pluto by the Romans. In addition to having three heads, Cerberus has a snake for a tail and other snakes growing out of his body. Hesiod wrote that he has fifty heads, which may or may not include the heads of the snakes. Cerberus is one of the offspring of Echidna and Typhon. He has a brother named Orthus, a two-headed dog. Orthus belongs to a three-headed giant named Geryon.

Cerberus ensures that no dead person can escape Hades nor can any living person enter. Nobody is capable of subduing him by force except for Hercules, the son of Zeus.

In his twelfth and final labor, Hercules was sent by King Eurystheus to retrieve Cerberus from the underworld and bring him to the palace. Hercules choked Cerberus unconscious, then bound him with iron chains and carried him back to the king. Eurystheus did not believe Hercules would complete this task. When he finally saw the beast he hid behind a pillar in fear. But all Cerberus wanted to do was go home, which he did as soon as he broke free. On a separate occasion, the legendary bard Orpheus lulled Cerberus to sleep with his magical lyre. Another hero named Aeneas once sedated the monstrous dog with an opium-laced honey cake.

CETUS

Cetus is the generic sea monster of Greek mythology. Originally called Ketos, the spelling and pronunciation of the beast's name were changed after being adopted by the Romans. Its female counterpart is Ceto. The terrifying creature is depicted as an enormous serpentine fish. It has a jagged sawtooth spine and may have multiple dorsal fins. Its face has mammalian characteristics, with large, sharp teeth and a long, pointed snout. As with other fish, its only limbs are two front fins. It is thought that the Greeks first imagined Cetus after catching glimpses of whales and large sharks in the sea. In ancient times these animals were highly mysterious, and their full appearance was unknown. The word *cetus* later came to mean whale in Latin. Whales and dolphins are scientifically known as *cetaceans*. Cetus is also a constellation in the night sky.

According to Greek legend, the god Poseidon deployed Cetus after being insulted by a mortal queen. Queen Cassiopeia of Ethiopia had bragged that her daughter, Andromeda, was more beautiful than Poseidon's daughters. Cetus proceeded to devour fishermen and sailors until the king and queen consulted an oracle. The oracle informed them that the only way to make Cetus go away was to sacrifice Andromeda to it as an offering. Remorsefully, they chained the princess to the cliffs in order to appease the monster and the gods. Luckily, the hero Perseus arrived just in time to rescue Andromeda. He killed Cetus, either with his sword or, in some versions, turning it to stone by showing it the severed head of Medusa. Perseus thus saved the kingdom and finally married Andromeda.

CHARYBDIS

Charybdis is a mysterious underwater monster infamous for producing gigantic whirlpools. She is said to be a daughter of Gaia and once looked human. Her father was either Poseidon or the primordial ocean god Pontus. Charybdis angered Zeus by serving Poseidon in a battle against him. In an alternative myth, she is said to have devoured cattle belonging to Hercules. Zeus struck her with a thunderbolt and cursed her to become bound to the bottom of the sea. Charybdis took on a massive, shapeless form, with flippers for limbs, and a mouth so large that she sucks in the sea every time she opens her jaws. Others are unsure of her true appearance, as she is never actually seen. Sometimes she is described as simply an enormous, disembodied mouth. Later writers identified Charybdis as the whirlpool itself.

In Homer's *Odyssey*, Charybdis is said to inhabit a narrow channel near another sea monster, Scylla. Scholars believe this channel to be the Strait of Messina, located between Italy and Sicily. Charybdis is located at one side of the strait and Scylla at the other, with less than the distance of an arrow's shot between them. Sailors must therefore choose which monster they would rather face, as there is not enough room to avoid them both. Odysseus and his men were mortified when they saw Charybdis swallow so much seawater that the sand at the ocean floor became visible. She then quickly belched it back out, sending up violent waves higher than the island crags. Reluctantly, they decided that Scylla was the safer option, despite her appetite for human flesh.

CHIMERA

The Chimera is one of the most fearsome monsters from Greek mythology. The beast is understood to be female, although she is depicted with a mane like a male lion. The word "chimerical" has come to describe any implausible composite of dissimilar things. Most classical renderings portray this lion-like monster as three-headed, with a goat's head growing from the middle of her back, and a snake's head at the end of her tail. Yet, the Chimera had only one head in her earliest known description, in Homer's *Iliad*. She was said to have the front half of a lion, the hindquarters of a she-goat, and the tail of a snake. In all descriptions, the Chimera is fire breathing and nearly impossible to defeat.

In the *Iliad*, King Iobates attempted to dispose of a young man named Bellerophon by assigning him to slay the Chimera. But Bellerophon was too smart to try to confront the beast like an ordinary foe. He consulted the Oracle and then tamed the legendary Pegasus. The flying horse allowed Bellerophon to hurl his spear down the Chimera's throat. The lead spear melted inside the monster's fiery maw, sealing up her windpipe and killing her. This epic battle supposedly took place on a volcano in Lycia, Anatolia. This volcano was referred to as Mount Chimera by the Romans. The Roman scholar Servius speculated that the volcano itself was the monstrous Chimera. He wrote that it has lions near its top, goats at the middle level, and snakes at its base. The volcano is fictional but is thought to have been inspired by a Lycian natural gas vent called Yanartas.

CROCOTTA

The crocotta of Ethiopia is a perplexing creature from ancient bestiaries. The earliest known record of this beast was written by Ctesias around 400 BCE. Ctesias does not describe the animal's appearance but implies a canine species, with its vernacular name, *cynolycos*, meaning dog-wolf. The crocotta is remarkably powerful, swift, and difficult to kill. It also has a voice that sounds like human speech. It preys on humans, deceiving its quarry by calling out their names.

Some later scholars have thought the crocotta to be an exaggerated interpretation of a hyena; hence the spotted hyena's scientific name, *Crocuta crocuta*. However, the Roman writers Pliny the Elder and Claudius Aelianus mentioned the crocotta and the hyena as separate species. Pliny believed the crocotta is born from the union of a hyena and a lioness. Pliny wrote that the deadly crocotta has no teeth, but singular ridges or blades of bone in its jaws with which it slices its prey.

Elsewhere, Pliny mentioned a creature called the leucrocotta, or "white crocotta." This appears to be the same animal as the crocotta, although Pliny did not state this explicitly. Like the crocotta, it has a ridge of bone in place of teeth, can imitate the human voice, and is the fastest animal in Ethiopia. Pliny describes the leucrocotta as having cloven hooves, a stag's haunches, a lion's neck and chest, and a badger's head. Its mouth extends as far back as its ears. Medieval Europeans occasionally included Pliny's leucrocotta (or leucrotta) in their bestiaries. Some modern writers have suggested that the leucrocotta is the offspring of a crocotta and a different animal.

CYCLOPS

A cyclops is a male humanoid giant with a large, single eye. The first three cyclopes in mythology were the children of Gaia and Uranus. The major gods of the Greek pantheon had not yet been born. Once the gods came into being, the three cyclopes forged weapons for them, including Zeus's thunderbolt and Poseidon's trident. Using these weapons, the gods were able to fight against the race of giants called the Titans and establish their dominance over the world. The cyclopes were also credited for building the massive "cyclopean walls" of ancient Mycenae. Eventually, the god Apollo killed the cyclopes to express his anger at Zeus. Some people speculate that the Greeks may have imagined these primordial beings after discovering the bones of extinct elephants.

A second generation of cyclopes later walked the earth. These were not the master masons and metalsmiths that the first cyclopes were. Instead they are portrayed as bumbling and brutish. In Homer's *Odyssey*, the hero Odysseus made landfall on an island inhabited by a cyclops named Polyphemus. Odysseus and his crew found Polyphemus's cave and snuck in to steal his food. Soon the cyclops came home from tending his sheep, whereupon he immediately ate two of the sailors. He sealed the rest of them inside the cave to eat later. The next time Polyphemus opened the cave, Odysseus offered him all the wine he was carrying on his ship. Foolishly, Polyphemus drank it all and passed out. While he was asleep, Odysseus and his men gouged out the giant's eye with a burning beam and escaped.

ECHIDNA

E chidna is a female monster whose name comes from the Greek word for viper. According to Hesiod, whose description of Echidna is the most frequently referenced, she has the upper body of a beautiful nymph and the lower body of a serpent. Alternatively, others have said she has a serpent's body from the neck down, or she has two serpents for legs, or she has a hundred heads. Echidna is infamously venomous and feeds on human flesh. Depending on the interpretation, she is either the daughter of the primordial ocean deities Ceto and Phorcys or of the water nymph Callirrhoe and a giant named Chrysaor. Despite having aquatic parents, Echidna was born in an underground cave. She lives in a palace inside the cave and guards a subterranean realm known as Arima.

Echidna is best known as the wife of Typhon and the mother of other monsters. Echidna and Typhon's many children include Cerberus, the Chimera, the hydra, the Greek sphinx, and a giant snake named Ladon. She also bore a two-headed dog named Orthus, which belongs to a three-headed giant named Geryon. She also produced the

Nemean lion, a great ravenous lion with special gold fur that serves as armor. Hesiod wrote that Echidna conceived the sphinx and the Nemean lion not from Typhon, but from her son, Orthus. Different authors have named Echidna as the mother of other monsters as well, sometimes contradicting other sources. These other monsters include Scylla, the Gorgons, the harpies, and other fearsome creatures from various myths. Eventually Echidna was killed by Argus Panoptes, a hundred-eyed giant who served the goddess Hera.

GORGON

As with several other Greek mythological beings, the Gorgons are a group of three. Their names are Stheno, Euryale, and Medusa. They are female but have a masculine appearance, sometimes even including a beard. They also have wings, large fangs, and snakes growing from their heads. The Gorgons' ugly faces, with large, staring eyes and lolling tongues, have been used as apotropaic symbols to ward off evil. Appearing very early in Greek artwork, they may have been influenced by mythology from farther east. According to one account, the Gorgons were once beautiful yet were turned into hideous monsters after they claimed to be finer looking than the gods. Some sources identify the Gorgons' parents as the sea monster Ceto and the sea god Phorcys. Others claim they are children of Typhon and Echidna.

Medusa is by far the most famous Gorgon and the only one of them who was mortal. Medusa was cursed by the goddess Athena after she had an affair with Poseidon inside Athena's temple. As a result, anyone who looked upon her face would be turned to stone. Some myths attribute this trait to all three Gorgons. Eventually, a king named Polydectes sent the hero Perseus to cut off Medusa's head. Perseus was able to accomplish this feat by using special gifts from various gods. These included an invisibility cap from Hades and a mirrored shield from Athena. Perseus never looked at Medusa directly, but only at her reflection in the shield. Medusa's face retained its power of petrification even after death. Perseus carried her head with him on subsequent adventures to use as a weapon against his enemies.

HARPY

The harpies have a divine origin in Greek mythology, yet they are portrayed as terrible, disgusting monsters. They are three nymphs, albeit unattractive ones, who personify violent winds. The name "harpy" means snatcher. Originally their role was to carry wicked people away to the Erinyes (Furies) for punishment. Depicted either as winged humans or as human-headed birds, the harpies are distinguished from the Sirens by their ugly faces. In later art, the bird-bodied form became more standard. They had the bodies of large vultures, and talons made of metal. They are filthy and foul smelling and their behavior is vile. Some sources attribute their origin to Typhon and Echidna, although this is not consistent with earlier myth.

The harpies are best known as the tormentors of Phineas, a king punished by Zeus. Blinded and exiled for misusing his power of prophecy, Phineas was banished to an island inhabited by the harpies. There was always enough food on the island, yet the former king had a difficult time eating any of it. The harpies constantly snatched the food out of his hands. Whatever was left on the table was usually spoiled by their vomit and excrement. Eventually Phineas was relieved by the hero Jason and his companions, the Argonauts. Two of the Argonauts were the sons of the North Wind and also had wings. Their names were Calais and Zetes, together known as the Boreades. These brothers chased the harpies all the way to the Strophades Islands. There, the harpies were protected by Iris, the goddess of rainbows. She forbade the Boreades from killing them, but the harpies never bothered Phineas again.

HIPPOCAMPUS

The horses that pull the chariot of Poseidon are known as the hippocampi, or "horse monsters." Poseidon is best known as the god of the sea, but he is also the god of travel, and, by extension, horses. In Roman mythology he is called Neptune. As an ocean god, his chariot is a seagoing vessel and his horses have the lower bodies of fish. Poseidon's daughters are sea nymphs called the Nereids, who are sometimes depicted riding on the hippocampi's backs. The creature is a literal sea horse, and therefore *Hippocampus* has become the scientific name of the real-life seahorse. The part of the brain called the hippocampus is so named because it is shaped like a seahorse.

A hippocampus can travel virtually anywhere. Unlike most marine animals, these creatures can inhabit fresh water as well as the sea. In the tale of Jason and the Argonauts, a great hippocampus emerged from the sea, assumed the shape of a normal horse, and went galloping across the Libyan Desert. Jason and his men picked up their boat and carried it as they followed the beast's trail, knowing it would lead them to more water.

Later renderings occasionally depicted the hippocampus as having wings in addition to a fish's tail. The creature became adopted into Phoenician, Etruscan, and medieval European art. After Greece became Christianized, the hippocampus appeared in an early bestiary called the *Physiologus*, under the name hydrippus, or "sea horse." The *Physiologus* made no mention of Poseidon from pagan religion but instead called the creature a Moses figure, claiming it leads all the other fish to their king.

HYDRA

The hydra, or Lernean hydra, is a many-headed serpent that once lurked in a Peloponnesian swampland called Lerna. Its breath is a deadly toxic gas, while its blood is capable of killing creatures that are otherwise said to be immortal. Traditionally, the hydra is depicted as having nine heads, although it can easily have more. Each time one head is chopped off, two more immediately grow back in its place. The only way to kill the hydra is to cut off all its heads, yet this is virtually impossible to do. In fact, one of the heads is immortal and supposedly cannot be severed. The creature was also accompanied by a large crab as a guard dog.

King Eurystheus assigned Hercules to slay the hydra for his second labor. Hercules was well prepared and brought with him his nephew Iolaus for assistance. The two of them wrapped cloths around their noses and mouths so they would not inhale the hydra's breath. Hercules wielded a special golden sword given to him by the goddess Athena, while Iolaus procured burning tree branches. Whenever Hercules would slice off one of the hydra's heads, he would immediately take one of the burning branches and cauterize the stump. This prevented the heads from growing back. Hercules was even able to sever the immortal head thanks to his special sword. He quickly trapped this head under a boulder so it could never harm anyone again. He killed the giant crab as well, which became the constellation Cancer. Finally, Hercules dipped his arrows in the hydra's blood, which would allow him to kill other dangerous beings in the future.

LAMIA

Lamia is a female monster who is notorious for devouring babies. She is typically envisioned as half human and half serpent, similar to Echidna. Earlier references suggest she had a more humanoid shape but with a grotesque face. She may have become imagined as half snake after being conflated with a gigantic female serpent named Sybaris. Some scholars have suggested that Lamia was originally a variant of the monstrous sea goddess Ceto, but others feel this connection is tenuous. Most sources associate her with the desert. Later European artists took liberties to further embellish Lamia's appearance. Her body may resemble other animals besides a snake, although she is always covered with scales and always has a woman's head and breasts.

According to legend, Lamia was formerly a beautiful woman who became the mistress of Zeus. This provoked the wrath of Hera, Zeus's wife. Hera cursed Lamia to become a monster and eat the children that she had with Zeus. Part of her transformation involved losing the ability to blink her eyes. In some versions of the myth, Zeus gave her relief by allowing her to remove her eyeballs from their sockets whenever she wanted. Some have tied this to the ability of prophecy. Before her transformation, Lamia had been a queen in Libya. This desert origin may reflect influence from Near Eastern folklore, as she bears similarities to the Hebrew Lilith. As with Lilith, Lamia is known as both a devourer of children and a deadly seductress. Later it was said that the *lamiai* are a race of seductive female demons, similar to the succubi from Christian folklore.

MANTICORE

Reputedly a Persian mythical creature, the manticore is known from the writings of Ctesias of Cnidus, who was Greek. He claimed it is shaped like a lion, red in color, with a human head and blue eyes. Within its mouth are three rows of sharp teeth. Its tail terminates in a series of venomous barbs, each up to a foot in length. These barbs can be shot out like darts for a distance of 100 feet in virtually any direction. They are soon replaced upon being discharged. The manticore is also said to have a voice like a trumpet yet is able to move without a sound. It is known as the fastest animal in the forest and is a relentless predator of humans. Manticores are rumored to live in India. Indian hunters ride on elephants to hunt this creature, as the elephant is the only animal that can withstand the venom of its darts.

Ctesias alleged to have learned of the manticore while he was serving at the court of the Persian king Ataxerxes Mnemon around 400 BCE. Suspiciously, however, the creature is not found in any known written legends from Persia or India. Its original name, *martikhora*, is derived from two historical Persian words meaning "man eater." Yet, Ctesias knew the Persian language, and it is entirely possible that he invented manticore himself. Later references to this beast were based directly on Ctesias's writings. Pausanias dismissed the poison barbs and triple rows of teeth and suggested that the manticore is actually a tiger. Nonetheless, the manticore survived into later European bestiaries and today is sometimes featured in fantasy games.

MEDUSA

—See *Gorgon*.

MINOTAUR

Half human and half bull, the Minotaur came into being after King Minos of Crete angered the gods with a lack of animal sacrifices. The god Poseidon had gifted Minos an extraordinary bull, expecting the king to soon sacrifice it back to him. Yet, Minos thought the animal was so beautiful that he decided to keep it for himself.

He sacrificed a lesser bull in its place, which the gods took as a brazen insult. Poseidon and Aphrodite teamed up and punished Minos by putting a curse on his wife, Pasiphae.

The queen suddenly fell madly in love with the bull from Poseidon. She seduced the bull by hiding herself inside a hollow wooden cow. As a result, she became pregnant with a half-animal monstrosity. The royal family hid their shameful offspring inside a labyrinthine dungeon underground. Every seven to nine years, the king would collect seven young men and seven young women from Athens and sacrifice them to the Minotaur.

A young man named Theseus, who was a demigod similar to Hercules, eventually volunteered himself for sacrifice. Theseus was supposedly stripped of his weapons, yet he managed to sneak in a sword that he hid under his tunic. He was also assisted by Minos's daughter, Ariadne, who had fallen in love with him. She gave him a ball of twine with which he was able to retrace his footsteps through the labyrinth. She also told him the layout of the labyrinth, as its designer, Daedalus, had described it to her. The hero was thus able to slay the Minotaur and escape from the labyrinth alive.

PEGASUS

Roman writers believed the Pegasus to be an exotic species that lives in faraway lands such as Ethiopia. Yet, in Greek literature, the generic term for a flying horse was *pterippus*. Pegasus was the name of a specific individual pterippus. This was a male specimen, pure white in color, sired by Poseidon. In earlier versions of the myth, Pegasus came into being when Medusa's blood mixed with the foam of the sea. In a later version he sprang forth from Medusa's neck after the hero Perseus beheaded her. Pegasus went to live on a sacred mountain called Mount Helicon, home to the Muses. There he stamped his hoof on the ground and magically produced a flowing spring. Called the Hippocrene, or "horse fountain," this spring is the mystical source of poetic inspiration.

Pegasus came into the possession of Athena, the goddess of war and wisdom. At one point, the young hero Bellerophon prayed to Athena for assistance in slaying the dreaded Chimera. He fell asleep in the Temple of Athena and awoke to discover a golden bridle in his hand. With it, he was able to capture Pegasus and successfully vanquish the Chimera. After his victory, Bellerophon brazenly attempted to fly Pegasus all the way to the top of Mount Olympus. Zeus, the king of the gods, decided that the pterippus was better suited for his own possession than the arrogant mortal's. He sent out a fly to bite Pegasus, which caused him to throw the young man off his back. To this day, Pegasus belongs to Zeus and is also a constellation in the night sky.

SATYR

The satyrs are an all-male race of nature spirits. "Satyr" is their Greek name; the Romans called them fauns. These beings are portrayed as humanoids with tails, while other aspects of their appearance may vary. Most of them have horns and some have goat legs. Goat-legged satyrs are called *panes* and are occasionally also portrayed with a goat head. They inhabit forests, rural countryside, and mountain wilderness. They are immortal beings, sometimes described as rustic gods.

Satyrs are closely associated with Dionysus, the god of wine and hedonism. Male chorus singers would traditionally dress up like these creatures during festivals of Dionysus. Satyrs also frequently appear in artwork depicting female devotees to Dionysus, called maenads. Other times they are portrayed lustfully chasing after forest nymphs. Satyrs are infamous for their insatiable sexual appetites, yet they are also associated with music.

One particularly famous satyr was named Pan. Most satyrs were not worshipped, yet Pan was revered by shepherds and hunters as the patron deity of animals. However, he would also instill outsiders with a sense of *panic* if they encroached upon his domain; hence the origin of the word. According to one myth, Pan lusted after a nymph named Syrinx. Syrinx had taken a vow of chastity and constantly fled from his advances. As Pan chased her through the woods, she prayed to Artemis for help to escape him. Finally, she was turned into a hollow reed plant. When Pan found the reed, he fashioned it into the musical instrument now known as the panpipes. Another satyr named Marsyas is also associated with musical instruments, especially the oboe and flute.

SCYLLA

Scylla is a horrific sea monster known for seizing sailors from ships. Once a beautiful naiad, or water nymph, she was transformed into a grotesque monstrosity after becoming caught in a love triangle. Some sources claim she had eyes for Poseidon, who in turn was desired by the sea goddess Amphitrite. Alternatively, she was the love of the primordial ocean god Glaucus and was cursed by the witch Circe. In both scenarios, the jealous rival poured a magic potion into the water near Scylla as she bathed. Classical Greek artwork portrays her as a mermaid with a serpentine tail and two dogs' heads and sets of forelegs growing from her waist. Her appearance is described differently in Homer's *Odyssey*. There, she is said to have twelve legs, six heads on long necks, and three rows of sharp teeth in each mouth. Homer did not mention dogs' heads but wrote that her voice sounds like dogs barking.

According to Homer, Scylla dwells within a narrow strait, which is possibly the Strait of Messina. She shares this channel with Charybdis. Any ship passing through must sail between the two monsters. Odysseus hoped that he could find Scylla and kill her before passing. He put on his armor and searched along the rocky cliffs but was unable to find her. He then continued sailing, trying his best to avoid the other monster, Charybdis. Suddenly, Scylla snuck up on the ship and plucked off six of the crew members. These men were worthy warriors, according to Odysseus, but their skills were of no use. Scylla disappeared with them underwater as quickly as she had emerged.

SIREN

Despite being confused with mermaids later on, the Sirens in Greek mythology are half bird. They were formerly a trio of young women who attended the young goddess Persephone. Persephone's mother, Demeter, had already given them wings, yet after Persephone was abducted by Hades, Demeter cursed them to become monsters. Roman writers identify the Sirens' home as a cluster of three small rocky islands called the *Sirenum scopuli*. There, they sing their enchanting songs as ships sail near the islands. The sailors become mesmerized by their spell until they crash their ship onto the rocks. Once ashore, the Sirens rip the men to shreds and devour them.

In Homer's *Odyssey*, the hero Odysseus is warned by the sorceress Circe that he will encounter the Sirens and other dangers at sea. Following Circe's advice, he ordered his men to stuff their ears with beeswax so they could not be seduced. But before they did this, Odysseus also had them tie him to the mast of the ship, without beeswax, so he could enjoy their song while they sailed past.

In the legend of Jason and the Argonauts, Jason was warned about the Sirens by the wise centaur Chiron. Per Chiron's advice, Jason recruited Orpheus to play his magical

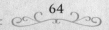

lyre as they sailed. When their ship approached the *Sirenum scopuli*, Orpheus produced a song that was louder and more beautiful than that of the Sirens. The Argonauts were thus able to pass the islands safely. In some versions of the myth, the Sirens are cursed to die if a man evades their spell, and thus Orpheus caused their death.

SPHINX, GREEK

The ancient Greeks learned of the legendary sphinx through their interactions with the Egyptians. Before long, the Greeks reinvented the creature into something much unlike its original form. They gave it wings, a feature not present in the Egyptian species. They also made it female, with a woman's head and breasts. Sophocles wrote that the sphinx has a serpent for a tail, although this does not appear in most images. She is said to be either the offspring of Typhon and Echidna, or of some incestuous combination of other members of Echidna's family. This reflects the evil nature of the Greek sphinx, which also distinguishes her from her Egyptian predecessor. The image of the Greek sphinx became the standard model in European artistic renderings of sphinxes.

One essential characteristic of the Greek sphinx is her infamous riddle. If her victims answer the riddle incorrectly, she gleefully mauls them to death. The riddle goes as follows: "What creature has a voice, four legs, then two legs, then three legs?" The answer is a human being. A person begins life by crawling on all fours, then walks on two legs, and in old age walks with a cane. Yet, most people assumed she was talking about some kind of monster and therefore could not guess the correct answer. The sphinx used this riddle to exterminate many residents of a city-state called Thebes. Eventually, a wandering Prince Oedipus from Corinth arrived and answered the riddle correctly. Reeling in defeat, the sphinx went mad and hurled herself off a cliff. Oedipus instantly became a hero and was named the new king of Thebes.

STYMPHALIAN BIRDS

The dangerous Stymphalian birds belong to Ares, the Greek god of war. They are portrayed in artwork as resembling common waterbirds such as cranes or geese, yet they have dagger-like beaks made of bronze. Later accounts also claim they have sharp feathers made of metal, which they can hurl like javelins. Ares's birds lived far away from humans until they relocated to escape from wolves. The birds settled at Lake Stymphalia in Arcadia, where they began multiplying uncontrollably. Before long, the invasive species took over the Arcadian countryside. There, they destroyed crops and, according to some versions of the myth, preyed on humans left and right. Their dung was also said to be poisonous.

King Eurystheus of Tiryns assigned the hero Hercules to rid Arcadia of the Stymphalian birds. Hercules sought the goddess Athena for aid. Athena in turn commissioned Hephaestus, the blacksmith god, to create a special set of metal castanets that could drive away the birds. With these castanets, Hercules was able to flush them out of hiding. Some sources claim the Stymphalian birds are immortal, yet it is often written that Hercules killed them by using arrows tipped with the poison of the hydra. Whether he killed them or not, Hercules successfully rid Arcadia of the deadly Stymphalian birds. Whatever birds survived fled to an island in the Euxine Sea. There they were subsequently encountered by Jason and the Argonauts. Jason's men managed to keep the birds off them by producing a loud commotion. One of the Argonauts was wounded by a feather, but nobody died.

TYPHON

Typhon, or Typhoeus, is the most powerful monster in Greek mythology. He is a primordial winged giant with a humanoid upper body and serpent tails in place of legs. Specific details of his appearance vary between accounts, including his number of serpentine legs and number of heads. Some sources describe him as having a hundred heads. He is also said to have serpents growing out of his shoulders, or even in place of fingers. All of these snakes hiss loudly and spit deadly venom. Typhon is so large that his head touches the stars. He embodies storms and volcanic eruptions. According to most sources, he was born to the earth goddess, Gaia. His father is usually identified as Tartarus, a personification of the dark abyss farther underground than Hades.

Long before mortals walked the earth, the Olympian gods went to war against a race of primordial giants called the Titans. This war was called the Titanomachy. The gods won and banished the Titans to the underworld of Tartarus. Gaia, the mother of the Titans, sought revenge. She produced Typhon, a monstrous son supposedly more powerful and terrifying than the gods themselves. Typhon rose up from underground through the caverns of Cicilia, Anatolia. Most of the gods fled in terror. Zeus faced the challenger one on one. There ensued a new battle just as intense as the Titanomachy. The whole world shook with Zeus's thunder and lightning, while Typhon generated fires, earthquakes, and devastating winds. In the end, Zeus trapped Typhon underneath Mount Etna, located in Sicily. The giant monster lives there to this day and is the cause of the volcano's activity.

Chapter Four

WESTERN EUROPE

Western Europe consists primarily of Germanic, Celtic, and Italic (Latin-based) cultures. This is in contrast with Eastern Europe, which is predominantly Slavic. During its historical development, Western Europe benefited from being in the same longitudinal trading zone as other civilizations of Eurasia. Westerners also gained a significant boost in mathematics and scholarly motivation due to Arab influence in the 1100s. This gave rise to the Renaissance period, which produced some of the greatest thinkers in the world at the time. Countries such as England, Spain, and France then began exploring the globe and establishing colonial empires. Today their descendants can be found all around the world. Unfortunately, Western imperialistic expansion also resulted in the destruction of countless indigenous cultures.

Western Europeans have been greatly fascinated with mythical creatures. Strange and fantastical beasts have appeared not only in folktales, but also in bestiaries and as heraldic symbols. Much of Western Europe's mythical inspiration is drawn from ancient Greece. This chapter places more emphasis on creatures that did not have a Greek origin. A great number of European mythical species are faeries and related beings, such as goblins, gnomes, and elves. This chapter minimizes this category in favor of a wider diversity of creatures. Christian beliefs shape many of the myths in this chapter, while Jewish folklore and pagan mythology are also present.

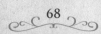

BAROMETZ

Also known as the vegetable lamb or Tartary lamb, the barometz is a lamb that grows on a tree or bush. This type of life form is referred to as a "zoophyte," or animal-plant. This strange organism appears in Renaissance bestiaries, travelers' tales, and rabbinical commentaries. The lamb is attached by its navel to the stalk of a large plant. It begins its life as a gourd, which opens up and develops a full animal shape. It feeds on grass but is limited by the length of the stem.

The barometz was purported to grow in the mountains of faraway lands, especially Tartary, which consists of eastern Russia and central Asia. It may come from a Russian word meaning "little ram." The oldest known references to the barometz suggest a Jewish origin of the myth.

The Hebrew word for barometz is *jeduah*. An early-thirteenth-century rabbi, Simeon of Sens, wrote that the jeduah is shaped like a person and will kill anyone who approaches it. In later writings the creature is generally agreed to be lamb-like and harmless. The monstrous jeduah and the lamb-like barometz may have originated as different myths from different regions and became conflated over time.

According to Jewish folklore, the bones of the barometz have magical properties and are ideal for divination. The creature is preyed upon by wolves and humans alike. Some sources claim that its flesh is as soft as fish and as sweet as honey. The barometz may have been inspired by the cotton shrub, *Gossypium*, which grows in parts of Africa and India as well as the Americas.

BEAST OF THE APOCALYPSE

There is more than one Beast associated with the Apocalypse in the Bible. The most infamous one is a seven-headed monster with ten horns. Each of its horns bears a crown. Its form is based on a leopard, yet it has the feet of a bear and the mouths of lions. This Beast is prophesized to emerge from the sea sometime before the Apocalypse. It will receive instruction from a seven-headed dragon, which is actually Satan. The Beast is a false prophet. People will marvel at it and worship it, ultimately bringing about the Final Judgment. A second, yet similarly subversive creature is foretold to emerge from the earth. This one is more obscure. It is only described as having the horns of a lamb and the voice of a dragon. These Beasts appeared to John, the narrator of the book of Revelation, in a vision from Jesus Christ.

It is generally understood that the Beast of the Apocalypse is a metaphor for a person or series of persons. The seven heads represent seven kings. Five of them have already passed, one was said to be currently ruling at the time the book of Revelation was written, and the other is yet to come. Notoriously, the number 666 is associated with it. Many historians feel that the passage was a commentary about the Roman Emperor Nero. The number 666 can be derived from the Hebrew spelling of Nero's name. More controversially, Seventh-Day Adventists have proposed that the Beast is actually the pope. Many believe the seventh head of the Beast is a person who has yet to reveal himself and may do so at any moment.

CALADRIUS

The caladrius is a magical bird from medieval bestiaries. It is pure white in color and resembles a cross between a duck and an egret. Although it looks like a mundane species, the caladrius is distinguished by its ability to diagnose and treat human illness. If it refuses to look at an ailing patient, it means the person is so sick that they are going to die. Yet if it looks straight at them, they can be saved. In many versions the caladrius itself can actually cure the person.

Legend states that Alexander the Great discovered this bird in its native Persia and was the first to recognize its medical potential. He imported it into Europe, where artwork depicts it in association with kings and nobility. Theoretically, a caladrius will offer its services to anyone, yet generally only royalty could afford to purchase it.

Folklore of the caladrius dates back to antiquity. The Greeks referred to it as the dhalion. This bird was introduced to medieval Europeans via the early Christian bestiary called the *Physiologus*. This text rendered various creatures in a religious light, the caladrius being a metaphor for Jesus Christ as savior. It claimed that the bird absorbs the sickness of a patient, thus curing them, and then flies up into the sunlight to be cleansed. Its feathers turn from white to gray after absorbing an illness, and then turn pure white again after bathing in the sun's rays. By late medieval times, some sources suggested that one must eat the caladrius in order to be cured. The meat of its thigh was especially effective in treating eye disorders.

COCKATRICE

—See *Basilisk*, chapter three.

DRAGON, EUROPEAN

The highly iconic European dragon arose from a more universal tradition of monstrous legendary serpents. The term for a giant mythical snake was *wurm* in Germanic folklore and *drakon* in ancient Greece. Eventually the "drakon" transitioned into a more distinctive monster that sported legs, deadly breath, and often wings. Evolving simultaneously, the northern Germanic *wurm* became the lindworm or lindorm. This species was depicted as having two legs but no wings. It was adopted into British heraldry as a creature called the wyvern, which had wings but was still only bipedal. The wyvern was said to kill its foes by using venom rather than fire. Fiery breath became more standard for European dragons over time and may be a product of Christian religious symbolism.

Contemporary media often portray dragons as cute and friendly. Historically, however, they were almost always antagonists, sometimes even a symbol of the devil. Because of this, Western European dragon myths usually involved heroic combat. Perhaps the quintessential example is the legend of Saint George, who was said to be a Roman soldier who converted to Christianity. During his exploits, he came to deliver the land of Silene (probably Cyrene) from a horrible, menacing dragon. This dragon ravaged the countryside before abducting the princess Alcyone, holding her captive in a cave. George wounded the dragon, and then he and the princess paraded it through town. Once they had drawn a crowd, he killed the beast. He then converted all the townsfolk to Christianity. Many scholars believe this account to be a Christian reinterpretation of the Greek myth of Perseus, who rescued Princess Andromeda from the sea monster Cetus.

GARGOYLE

In popular culture today, people tend to think of gargoyles as a race of humanoid monsters, often sporting leathery wings. However, the gargoyle actually originated as an offshoot of the European dragon. The term also refers to a type of architectural carving or statue representing a grotesque creature. All three of these visions of the gargoyle are concurrent with one another. It began with a legend taking place near the Seine River in France. This region was terrorized by a dragon in early medieval times. The dragon, named La Gargouille, had the power to unleash floodwaters in addition to breathing fire. Eventually, it was killed by the heroic Saint Romanus. The saint decapitated the creature and mounted its head and neck onto the outer wall of a church in Rouen.

The gargoyle rapidly evolved into a broad class of legendary creature. Some stone gargoyles in Europe, especially France, resemble the dragon killed by Saint Romanus. Yet others took on an unlimited variety of shapes. Some resemble natural animals, such as lions, deriving from an older tradition of using animal statues as downspouts. Many others appear as combinations of different species, and a great number of them have humanoid features. Ultimately the gargoyle is defined by its role, rather than its appearance. Architecturally, gargoyle statues contain drain pipes that release rain water through the mouth. *Gargouille* means throat in Old French and is related to the word "gargle." The statues traditionally appeared on Catholic churches. They were meant to depict the concept of evil; hence their generally demonic appearance. Later they came to be seen as protectors of buildings.

 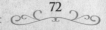

GOBLIN

The goblins are a class among the Fair Folk, or faeries. They are one of the most famous classes, as well as one of the most monstrous or grotesque. They are tiny in stature and extremely ugly. Historically they were envisioned as being hairy. Today they are usually depicted with green skin and long, pointy ears. Goblins and their cultural equivalents appear in the folklore of several European countries, including the United Kingdom, France, and Germany. In Scotland they are identified with the Unseelie Court of faeries, which includes all faerie races that are dark and chaotic. According to Welsh folklore, the tribe of goblins is ruled by the faerie king, Gwyn ap Nudd. The goblins themselves are low in rank.

Some writers simply define goblins as any kind of faerie that is malevolent in nature. Being defined so broadly, there are numerous variants from different regions. Generally speaking, goblins are mischievous and uncouth, although usually not dangerous. Only certain varieties are a particular cause for alarm. Notably, the redcap of the United Kingdom kills its victims and dyes its hat with their blood. The less dangerous ones are sometimes called hobgoblins.

Goblins live in a variety of places. Some are found in human dwellings, where they remain unseen, but are infamous for playing pranks. In French folklore they are thought to live outdoors. There, too, they are invisible but may pinch or otherwise harass people who travel alone at night. The German goblin is called a kobold and is typically thought to haunt mines underground. The mineral cobalt is named after this creature.

GRENDEL

Grendel is a monster from the famous Anglo-Saxon epic poem *Beowulf*. This work was penned approximately a thousand years ago by an unknown author. It identifies Grendel and other monsters as the descendants of the biblical Cain. Grendel's appearance is never clearly described, thus giving the readers much liberty in imagining his form. It is only specified that his skin is covered with hard, spiky scales that cannot be pierced with a sword. Otherwise he is enormous in size, walks on two legs, and is extremely ugly. Grendel lives in a dark swamp alone with his mother. He is a miserable creature, shunning sunlight and loathing humans. *Grendel*, a 1971 novel by John Gardner, richly illustrates the monster's life as one of nihilistic despair.

The epic of *Beowulf* begins after Grendel has repeatedly terrorized a Danish festival hall called Heorot. Infuriated by the joy of the party guests, the monster would wait until nightfall and then kill the guests as they slept. King Hrothgar, the host of the festivals, summoned the hero Beowulf for aid. Beowulf was a man graced with superhuman strength. His retainers first attacked Grendel with swords, yet their weapons were ineffective. Beowulf then fought the monster barehanded. He managed to grab the fiend's arm and tear it out of its socket. Defeated, Grendel fled back to his swampy lair, where he died. Seeking revenge, Grendel's mother attacked Heorot the following night. Beowulf followed her back to her lair, where he found a monster-sized sword too heavy for ordinary men to lift. With this he killed Grendel's mother and also decapitated Grendel's corpse.

GRIFFIN

The griffin is a very ancient mythical creature. It did not originally come from Western Europe, but it is difficult to determine precisely where it was conceived. Eventually, the Greeks learned about griffins in their travels afar. The majestic creatures were purported to live in India and other distant lands. They were said to guard natural deposits of gold, mine it with their beaks, and even line their nests with it.

Preserved in classical literature, the griffin became adopted both into Eastern and Western European folklore but has been more prominent in the latter. Sir John Mandeville wrote that one griffin is as strong as eight lions and as brave as one hundred eagles. Lions and eagles were symbols of royalty and power in Western Europe. Thus the griffin appeared on coats of arms as an emblem of strength and courage. In British heraldry, only the female griffins have wings. The wingless males have a spiky appearance.

The combination of lion and eagle was also interpreted to have religious significance, symbolizing the corporeal and heavenly aspects of the divine. According to an early Christian bestiary called the *Physiologus*, two griffins follow the sun through the sky.

One represents the Archangel Michael; the other, the Virgin Mary. One medieval legend states that Alexander the Great had managed to subdue a pair of griffins and kept them chained to his throne. He eventually became so arrogant that he made the creatures carry him upward into the sky. Yet when Alexander looked into the eye of Heaven, he realized that he is only mortal and quickly retreated to earth.

HIPPOGRIFF

Its name meaning "horse-griffin" in Greek, the hippogriff is a hybrid of griffin and horse. This crossbreed has an equine body with talons for its front feet, as well as eagle wings and an eagle head with pointed ears. It lacks any visible characteristic of the lion as seen in the standard griffin. The hippogriff originated as a depiction of irony. Griffins were reputed to prey on horses, not breed with them. The Roman poet Virgil wrote, "Griffins will now be mated with horses" to signify an impossible event. The most absurd scenario imagined was an offspring born of a male griffin and a female horse. Even if such an unlikely coupling occurred, it was thought that the creature would never be born because the griffin would devour the horse before it could give birth.

Despite the mocking attitude held in antiquity, the hippogriff was given a second life during the Renaissance period. One of these creatures appeared in Ludovico Ariosto's epic poem, *Orlando Furioso*, from 1516. The hippogriff in this story was born to a male griffin and a female horse in a distant land called Ryfee. It was tamed by a magician named Atlante and then passed on to a knight named Rogero. Rogero rode the hippogriff across the entire known world to rescue a fair damsel named Angelica. Earlier in the story, Angelica had spurned her former lover, Orlando, which caused him to go mad. Another knight named Astolfo would later ride the hippogriff around the world in search of a cure for Orlando's madness. Astolfo was eventually successful and afterward set the hippogriff free.

KELPIE

The kelpie is an evil aquatic shapeshifter that can assume the form of a horse. Its name is Scottish, although similar monsters are found in the folklore of other countries. Other variants include the ceffyl dŵr in Wales, the nykur in Iceland, and the bäckahäst in Scandinavia. This deadly being is associated with the faerie realm, with the surface of the water serving as the boundary between two worlds.

The kelpie's true form beneath the water is unknown. Above water it usually looks like an ordinary horse, although in some regions it is said to have unusual features, such as backward hooves or a mane of snakes. It is also capable of speech. Sometimes it assumes a human shape. The kelpie is infamous for waiting by a road and posing as an ordinary horse, already equipped with a saddle and tack. It tricks people into riding it and then immediately dives back into the water, drowning its victim. Sometimes kelpies may sing an enchanting song to lure their prey. They are also able to raise floods and create thunderstorms. Occasionally they transform into men and seduce women or assault passersby.

A person can gain power over a kelpie by cutting off its bridle. According to one Scottish legend, this was done by a laird named Graham of Morphie. Once he had the animal under his command, he forced it to move stones for him to build a castle. He worked the creature nearly to death. Upon completion he returned the kelpie's bridle. The kelpie then cursed the laird and his entire lineage. Eventually Graham's family line completely died out.

KRAKEN

The kraken originated in Norwegian folklore. In modern times this sea monster is envisioned as a gargantuan octopus or squid. The real-life giant squid, which may exceed 40 feet in length, is often presumed to be the basis of the myth. The giant squid is relatively harmless; nonetheless, beached remains and tentacles found in the bellies of whales may well have fueled the legend of the kraken.

The earliest depictions and descriptions of the fantastic beast were vague with regard to its species. Some older interpretations suggest something more like a crab than a squid. The kraken is traditionally said to be so large that its body can be mistaken for an island. When it submerges quickly it creates a massive whirlpool in its wake. Later, the creature was depicted as being smaller than an island, yet still large enough to grapple with ships.

Some eighteenth-century naturalists took the kraken seriously. These include the famous Swedish biologist Carolus Linnaeus, who listed the creature in one of his earlier works in 1735. He classified it as a cephalopod and gave it the scientific name *Microcosmus marinus*. The French zoologist Pierre Dénys de Monfort suggested that the kraken or colossal octopus was responsible for sinking ships. The kraken was also described extensively in 1752 by the Danish bishop Erik Pontoppidan in *The Natural History of Norway*. Pontoppidian believed the beast had a width of one and a half miles. He wrote that it sits at the bottom of the sea, eating fish and producing droppings. The sea monster's dung smells of fish and serves as bait that lures in more fish.

KRAMPUS

—See *Karakondzho*, chapter five.

LOCH NESS MONSTER

The monster of Loch Ness, Scotland, has become the most famous cryptid lake monster in the world. Folklore of a monster in Loch Ness has existed for centuries, although for most of history it was known only on a local scale. The creature was probably originally a form of kelpie. Many sources cite the story of Saint Columba as the first written account of the Loch Ness monster. Dated to around 565 CE, the account does not actually take place at Loch Ness, but on the nearby River Ness. Allegedly, a savage "water beast" attacked and killed a man who was swimming in the river. The monster prepared to claim a second victim, but Saint Columba intervened. He made the sign of the cross and commanded the beast to go back at once. The creature suddenly moved backward as though being pulled by an unseen hand.

The Loch Ness monster, or Nessie, as it would soon be called, did not become widely known until a series of sightings were reported in 1933. An explosion of sightings followed and persisted for decades. Descriptions varied, yet the monster is widely agreed to have a long neck and small head. Occasionally it was sighted on dry land. There have been several supposed photographs and even video footage of the creature. Cryptozoologists have proposed various theories as to what kind of animal Nessie may be. These include a giant eel, a plesiosaur, a long-necked mammal, and even a massive invertebrate. The monster brought a boost in tourism to Loch Ness and sparked multiple investigations. Sightings have significantly declined in recent years.

MERMAID

Mermaids and similar beings are found in folklore all around the world. The Western European version is almost exclusively ocean dwelling, whereas versions from other cultures often inhabit fresh water. The word "mermaid," means sea maiden. The male equivalent, called a merman, is known but seldom mentioned in western European lore. Renowned for their beauty, European mermaids are associated with love and passion. Sailors would occasionally report seeing them after being out at sea for long periods. In some folktales, mermaids can assume full human shape in order to seduce men. Perhaps due to influence from the Greek Siren, these beings sometimes appear as an omen of storms and other misfortunes. Mermaids are also notorious for falling in love with human sailors and dragging them underwater, causing them to drown.

One famous Western European story about a mermaid is Hans Christian Andersen's fairy tale *The Little Mermaid*, published in Denmark in 1837. The mermaid protagonist in this story falls in love with a human prince. Instead of drowning him, however, she saves him from being drowned. This tale has been adapted into a Disney animated movie, but the original version was much darker. The Little Mermaid asks a Sea Witch to make her human so she can marry the prince and have an immortal soul. In so doing, she sacrifices her beautiful voice and is cursed to feel excruciating pain with every step she takes. Tragically, the prince marries a different woman. The Sea Witch allows the Little Mermaid to return to the sea if she kills the prince with a knife. Instead, the Little Mermaid uses the knife to kill herself.

PELUDA

The Peluda is a bizarre and horrific monster said to have terrorized the French town of La Ferté-Bernard. Its name means "shaggy one" in the Occitan language. It is called La Velue in French. This unique monstrosity has a massive body covered in sharp quills. Its head, neck, and tail resemble a snake's, while its feet are those of a turtle. Its overall size is like an ox, but some accounts say it is much larger. Its quills are green, resembling vegetation. These quills can lie limp like hair, move like tendrils, or stiffen into sharp, deadly spines. The Peluda is capable of shooting these spines out like arrows. It can also breathe fire, spit venom, and exhale toxic vapor that withers crops. When it takes to the river, its evil power raises a flood.

The Peluda existed at the time of the Great Flood. It was rejected from Noah's Ark, yet it survived the deluge. It then slept dormant in a cave near the Huisine River for thousands of years, finally reawakening in medieval times. The beast roamed the countryside of La Ferté-Bernard, destroying crops and livestock. Eventually, it began eating women and children. One brave young man who suffered the loss of his beloved consulted the village wise woman for advice. The wise woman informed him that the Peluda's only vulnerable spot is its tail. The young man then donned a suit of mail and went out to slay the creature. Its stinging spines could not pierce his armor, and finally he hacked off its tail. The townspeople of La Ferté-Bernard embalmed the Peluda and rejoiced.

PHOENIX

—See chapter six.

QUESTING BEAST

The Questing Beast is a monster from Arthurian legend. It is usually said to have the head and neck of a snake, the body of a leopard, the hindquarters of a lion, and the hooves of a deer. Its most significant and consistent characteristic is the sound it makes: a clamor like dozens of barking dogs tearing apart its quarry. This is the basis of its name. It is also called the Bête Glatissant, or "barking beast," in French. Its English name has a dual meaning, as the creature is also quested after. Some Old French texts suggest that the monster's distinctive sound is actually produced by the beast's offspring inside its womb. The furious whelps tear the animal apart from the inside, symbolizing moral corruption and impiety within the kingdom. The Questing Beast represents the degeneration and sin that will eventually lead to the kingdom's demise. It is continually pursued by various knights errant but always eludes defeat.

Perhaps the most dramatic account of the Questing Beast is described in the *Suite du Merlin*, a book from the post-Vulgate cycle. In this version, the creature is the offspring of a corrupted princess who consorted with the devil. This princess lusted after her own brother but was unsuccessful in seducing him. The devil then persuaded her to accuse her brother of rape. The king responded to the accusation by sentencing his son to be killed by a pack of hounds. In his final words, the wrongly convicted prince cursed his sister to give birth to an abomination. The beast's distinctive call would serve as a grim reminder of his unjust death.

SALAMANDER

The mythical salamander closely resembles an ordinary lizard and shares its name with a real-life amphibian. It is frequently imagined as red in color, sometimes with star-shaped markings on its back. In some interpretations it has more-embellished features, such as a mammalian-looking head or a dragon-like appearance. It is generally thought to be small.

One of the foremost qualities of the salamander is its resistance to fire. Pliny the Elder wrote that salamanders seek fire, yet are so cold that they extinguish the flames upon entry. Contrastingly, the Talmud states that these creatures are generated by fire. Leonardo da Vinci wrote that salamanders cannot eat food, as they lack any digestive organs, and instead depend on fire for sustenance. Alchemists used the salamander to symbolize the mineral sulfur. The sixteenth-century physician Paracelsus declared the salamander to be the fire elemental.

The salamander's other principal characteristic is its toxicity. The creature produces a white, milky venom, which it either secretes from its skin or can spit from its mouth as a weapon. This substance causes anything it comes in contact with to corrode. Some believed that anything a salamander touches would in turn become lethally toxic. If it climbs a tree, the tree's fruit will become poisonous. Salamanders were also rumored to produce a white silk or wool from their bodies, which becomes purified when placed in fire. Alleged samples of this wool were imported to Europe from India, supposedly coming from the legendary kingdom of Prester John. "Salamander wool" has since been identified as asbestos, a mineral substance that is fire resistant and also poisonous.

SEA SERPENT

Western Europeans traditionally imagined that the deep sea is inhabited by gigantic serpentine beasts. Sea serpents are not limited to western European folklore, yet they are prevalent in it, whereas sea monsters from other continents frequently resemble other animals. Even in modern day, Western cryptozoologists have wondered if sea serpents may be real animals unknown to science. Numerous people have reported seeing sea serpents over the centuries. One of the most famous sightings was reported in 1848 by the crew of the British warship HMS *Daedalus*. The creature was observed very close to the ship and was estimated to be 60 feet long. Skeptics believe that the sailors actually saw a baleen whale. Other sightings may be explained by several dolphins swimming in a straight line, or other mundane animals such as oarfish. Decomposing basking sharks have been mistaken for sea serpent carcasses.

Sea serpent folklore was probably influenced by the Judeo-Christian Leviathan. However, sea serpent myths also existed in Europe prior to the introduction of Christianity. One example is Jörmungandr, the Midgard Serpent from Norse mythology. This serpent is so enormous that it encircles the entire world. Long ago, the god Thor drew up Jörmungandr on a gigantic fishing line and intended to kill the beast. This terrified the primordial giant Hymir, who quickly intercepted Thor's attempt by cutting the line. Jörmungandr thus returned to the bottom of the sea. The Midgard Serpent will rise up again at the end of time, known as Ragnarok. At that time, Thor is destined to slay Jörmungandr. Thor himself will also die immediately afterward, being poisoned by the serpent's venom.

SLEIPNIR

Odin, the most powerful of the Norse gods, rides on the back of a fantastic horse named Sleipnir. Rather than having wings like numerous other prominent mythical horses, Sleipnir is distinguished by having eight legs. Named the Sliding One, this stallion is the fastest horse in the universe. He was even able to outrun Gullfaxi, the fabulous golden-maned horse belonging to a giant named Hrungnir. He is also able to travel to realms that are inaccessible by any other mount. Odin rides him to all the Nine Worlds, including Hel, the underworld, and Jotunheim, the land of the giants. Due to his world-crossing abilities, Sleipnir is sometimes described as a shamanic horse.

Sleipnir's father was a mason's workhorse named Svadilfari. The gods of Asgard had commissioned the mason to build a great stone wall around their realm. The mason demanded the sun, the moon, and the goddess Freyja as payment for his labor. The gods insisted that they would only pay him this ridiculous sum if he completed the project in six months' time. However, Svadilfari was such an exceptional workhorse that the mason was able to build the wall at an alarming rate. The gods became concerned.

Finally, the god Loki intervened by distracting Svadilfari. Loki transformed himself into a mare and lured the stallion away from his work. They were gone together long enough that the mason missed his deadline. Loki became pregnant and would later give birth to the foal Sleipnir. Meanwhile, the gods discovered that the mason was actually a giant, thereupon which Thor killed him with his hammer.

TARASQUE

The Tarasque is named for the French town of Tarascon, or perhaps the reverse. The earliest version of this creature was actually a European dragon, and as such it was described in *The Golden Legend* from around 1260. Later it evolved into a six-legged monster with the feet of a bear. It had the head of a lion and the tail of a serpent, armed with a sharp point or stinger at the end. Protecting its back was a tortoise-like shell covered with spikes.

The Tarasque was sired by the biblical Leviathan and born to a land-dwelling beast called the bonacho, or bonnacon. The bonnacon resembles a bison and produces dangerous flaming excrement. Born in Anatolia, the Tarasque migrated to Tarascon, which was then called Nerluc. There it lurked near the River Rhone, where it fed on livestock and soon began preying on humans. The king sent out sixteen brave knights to put an end to the Tarasque. Eight of the knights were killed by its fiery breath, and the others fled in terror.

The Tarasque continued to claim more victims until Martha of Bethany arrived in Nerluc. The fair woman, a personal friend of Jesus Christ, approached the monster as it was absorbed in its latest meal. The moment it reared its ugly head, she held up two branches in the shape of a cross. The Tarasque suddenly froze. Saint Martha then splashed its head with holy water, causing it to become tame. Triumphant, she led the pacified beast through town on a leash. The townspeople reacted by relentlessly attacking the Tarasque and soon stoned it to death.

TATZELWURM

Throughout the Alps are rumors of a lizard-like creature called the tatzelwurm. It has various other names across different localities, such as the stollenwurm ("burrowing worm"), springewurm ("jumping worm"), and bergstutzen ("mountain stump"). Tatzelwurm is its most famous name, meaning "worm with feet" in German. Historically the word "worm" referred to any serpent and suggests a common ancestry with the European dragon. The tatzelwurm is a reptile around 2–5 feet in length, with a thick body, short neck, and short limbs. It is usually said to have only two front legs, although some assume it to be four legged. Its head is triangular and has the eyes of a cat. It is also said to have impenetrable skin and a venomous bite.

Numerous cryptozoologists have eyed the tatzelwurm as a species of lizard that may actually exist. However, cryptozoologists often disregard the more fantastical descriptions of the creature, in which it is said to have the head of a cat and the body of a snake or dragon. At least one account claims it has green blood that burns human flesh.

Rather than being known since time immemorial, the tatzelwurm rose to fame in 1779. An Austrian man named Hans Fuchs reported encountering a pair of the creatures that year. The incident terrified him so badly that he went mad. Shortly afterward he suffered a fatal heart attack. Tatzelwurm folklore became popular following this story, particularly in Austria and Switzerland. The creature appeared in many nineteenth-century almanacs but was never officially regarded as a real animal. There have been multiple tatzelwurm hoaxes.

TROLL

Trolls are a class of humanoid monster originating in Scandinavian folklore. These beings are often portrayed with an enlarged nose and ears, long arms, and a hunched shape. Sometimes they are also given animalistic traits such as horns, hair all over their body, tusks, or a tail. In most regions, trolls are said to be much larger than humans, although in Sweden they are often smaller. Trolls may dwell in caves, under hills, or beneath bridges. They are usually portrayed in a negative light and are often said to eat people. They are very similar to ogres from English folklore. As with ogres, trolls are known to be extremely strong but not very smart. They are also similar to the faerie folk, as they are close to nature and considered otherworldly or magical.

The earliest mention of trolls comes from ancient Norse literature. They were originally a type of rustic giant yet were distinct from the standard Norse giants called Jötnar. Over time, trolls evolved into a myriad of forms in different regions. Some versions are able to pass as humans, possibly by using magic to disguise themselves. In Denmark these shapeshifting creatures are very much like malevolent faeries. They may assume the form of a very attractive man or woman in the middle of the woods. After gaining a human's trust, the troll may wreak havoc in the person's home, much as goblins do. Like other humanoid monsters around the world, trolls have been blamed for stealing human babies and replacing them with ill-fated changelings. Some folktales claim that trolls will turn into stone when exposed to sunlight.

UNICORN

One of the most iconic mythical creatures in the world, the unicorn has become synonymous with fantasy itself. It is thought to have evolved from the karkadann of Persia, and from the Indian ass and cartazonus described by Roman scholars. Well into the Renaissance, Europeans spoke of unicorns allegedly living in distant countries. These may have actually been references to rhinos and other real animals.

One of the oldest known facts about this creature is that its horn can cure poison. Narwhal tusks were sometimes passed off as unicorn horns, called alicorns, and sold for their supposed magical powers. Because of its horn, the unicorn became regarded as the ultimate prize for hunters. The animal was impossible to catch unless it happened upon a female virgin. According to the *Physiologus*, unicorns are drawn to the innocence of virgins and will rest their head in a young woman's lap. The creatures became associated with moral purity and were therefore depicted as pure white in color.

Although today it is envisioned as gentle and friendly, historically the unicorn was considered fierce. In Christian literature the creature was known for its indomitable spirit. Medieval writings mention Alexander the Great fighting against a herd of unicorns and also suggest that his horse was one. In Great Britain the beast was often portrayed as the natural enemy of the lion. The lion was more powerful in the summertime, yet the unicorn would return to dominate the forest in the spring. The unicorn became the heraldic emblem of Scotland, and the lion of England, with their rivalry serving as an allegory for the two countries' political relationship.

WEREWOLF

The concept of a werewolf is known throughout Europe, both Western and Eastern. The traditional werewolf was simply a person who transforms into a wolf, voluntarily or otherwise. This phenomenon, called lycanthropy, has been described since ancient times. Werewolves first appear in literature by the ancient Greeks and Romans. Yet, classical writers were not necessarily the inventors of this myth, as tales of lycanthropy also existed in the oral traditions of nonliterate communities. Lycanthropy may have its roots in shamanic beliefs from tribal societies. It became regarded as a curse after the spread of Christianity.

Characteristics of werewolves have varied tremendously over time and between different regions. The standard narrative recognized today, including the belief that werewolves can only be killed by silver bullets, is of recent origin. Between the fifteenth and eighteenth centuries, Europeans persecuted supposed werewolves similarly to how they hunted witches. Belief in these beings was prevalent in Germany, Scandinavia, Switzerland, France, and Eastern Europe. A multitude of unusual characteristics could mark a person as a potential werewolf. Suspects were often accused of cannibalism, and some of them were actually murderers.

One of the most infamous werewolf cases comes from a region of France then known as Gévaudan, today called Lozère. Between 1764 and 1767, a large wolf-like beast allegedly killed around one hundred people and injured many others. There was a gap in attacks in 1766, which folklore attributes to a man having been arrested and held in custody. The werewolf resumed his rampage after he was let out or escaped. The story of the Beast of Gévaudan has been retold and further embellished in numerous sources.

WOLPERTINGER

The alpine forests of Bavaria, Germany, are said to be haunted by a ferocious little animal called the wolpertinger. Descriptions of this creature vary, yet it is typically envisioned as rabbit-like with antlers, wings, and large fangs. Like the American jackalope, taxidermists craft wolpertingers by sewing parts of different animals together. These beastly creations do not all look alike, as tradition allows taxidermists to use their own creative license. The creature's body is always mammalian but is not necessarily rabbit based. It may be made from a squirrel, fox, or other small animal. Some specimens have the feet of a chicken or other bird.

The concept of the wolpertinger is meant to be comically absurd. Folklore dictates that the only way to catch one is to lure it with an attractive woman. Once the creature approaches, the woman must lift her shirt and expose her breasts. The creature becomes so excited that it faints, thus allowing it to be captured.

The wolpertinger is one of several similar creatures known throughout northern Europe. Various regions have their own absurdist mascot that serves a similar role. A nearly identical monster called the rauracki is said to dwell in Austria. An antlered rabbit called the rasselbock is said to live in the Thuringian Forest in Germany, while a winged hare called the skvader is known in Sweden. The Palatinate region of Germany is home to the legendary elwedritsche, which is shaped like a chicken or grouse with antlers. The wolpertinger is the most famous out of all of these, yet any of them may appear as taxidermic mounts, statues, and postcards in their respective localities.

Chapter Five

EASTERN EUROPE AND CENTRAL EURASIA

This chapter transcends the arbitrary divide between Europe and Asia, encompassing an enormous area of land on a singular continent. Major cultural groups in this region include the Slavic peoples, Turks and Tatars, Uralic language speakers, Mongols, and various Siberian tribes. Historically, the expansive steppes of central Asia were dominated by equestrian nomads, including the Scythians and the Huns. These cultures produced some of the most formidable warriors of ancient times. Russia controls much of this space today and claims the greatest land area out of any nation in the world. It had even more land from 1922 to 1991, when it was the Union of Soviet Socialist Republics (USSR), or Soviet Union. This giant rivaled the United States as a world superpower.

Humanoids with animal features, such as fur and horns, are remarkably common in Eastern European and central Asian folklore. Many of these fall under the broader umbrella of faeries, a category also prominent in Western Europe. Due to this overlap, faerie-like creatures are downplayed in this chapter, in favor of others that are more bestial. The most well-known mythical creatures in this region come from the Slavic countries of Eastern Europe. Myths from east of the Ural Mountains are generally less accessible to Westerners. This is partly due to a lower population density in Siberia, but information is also limited to the West because of political tensions with Russia.

AITVARAS

The aitvaras is a magical shapeshifting creature from Lithuania. It is known as a household spirit and typically commits itself to a particular domicile. Most of the time this creature appears as a rooster, usually a black one but sometimes white. It is sometimes imagined as having a fiery tail. At night it transforms into a tiny fiery serpent and takes to the air. Flitting around the village at high speeds, it appears only as a fast-moving fireball to the human eye. When at rest it looks like an ordinary rooster. The aitvaras' Latvian counterpart is called the pukis or puk. This creature's role and abilities are virtually identical to the aitvaras except that its daytime form is a cat.

The aitvaras is known as a wish-granting bird. Its purpose is to acquire goods for its master, such as grain and other foods, as well as gold. Typically this means it steals from other people. At home the aitvaras protects its master's belongings. However, it also brings misfortune, as the legend teaches people to be careful what they wish for. People who have an aitvaras always end up deeply regretting that they got it, as they learn all too late that their selfishness has brought them great misery. Yet once an aitvaras has been committed to a particular house, it is very difficult to make it leave. Many people say the aitvaras is obtained by bartering one's own soul to the devil. The creature originates by hatching from an anomalous rooster's egg, like a basilisk. Upon its death it becomes a spark.

AK BARS

The Ak Bars, or Aq Bars, is the official symbol of the Republic of Tatarstan, a federated state in eastern Russia. Its name means white leopard in Tatar. Its modern depiction is a winged, pure-white leopard with no spots, as it appears on the Tatarstan state coat of arms. Historically, the Ak Bars was a symbol of Volga Bulgaria, an ancient kingdom from which modern Tatars claim descent. Tatarstan chose it for their national emblem in 1991 to assert their identification with their historic past as Turkic Bulgars instead of with their Russian conquerors. Tatarstan did not succeed in gaining independence from Russia; nonetheless, the Ak Bars remains on their seal. A similar animal appears on the Khakassia coat of arms in Siberia.

Little is known about the original symbolic significance of the Ak Bars, other than that it is believed to be a tribal totem from an ancient religion called Tengriism. The word *ak* means white, and *bars* refers to a snow leopard (*Panthera uncia*). The snow leopard is notably associated with the Barsils, a Turkic tribe who lived near the Volga River. Barsil means "snow leopard people" in Tatar.

Today there are several companies in Tatarstan named Ak Bars, including the professional hockey team of Kazan, Tatarstan's capital. In some cases it is unclear whether "Ak Bars" refers to a mythical winged, pure-white feline or simply a common snow leopard. The hockey team's logo depicts a common snow leopard, yet the state seal with the winged version also appears on their jerseys. Some artists depict the Ak Bars as having both spots and wings.

AL

The evil spirit called the al, hal, or xal is known from the Caucasus region of central Asia, southern Russia, and Iran. It is especially prevalent in Armenian folklore. Als are usually regarded as female, although male ones also exist. These grotesque humanoids typically appear as hideous old hags with wild hair and long, sagging breasts. They may have fiery eyes, copper claws, iron fangs, tusks like a boar, and a nose made of clay. There are numerous regional variations of this monster. Some versions can pass for human, while others are half animal. They are often thought to be red in color, as *al* means red in the Turkic languages. Als are also said to live underwater.

Despite its many variations, the al consistently preys on pregnant women, fetuses, mothers in childbirth, and newborn babies. The evil creature kills its victims by stealing their liver, lungs, or heart. It is often imagined as carrying a pair of scissors, although it can actually remove organs without causing any open wounds. The al can destroy a person's soul by taking their liver, as the liver is believed to contain the soul. The al may also replace newborn babies with changelings that are fated to die within a few days. Pregnant women may keep the monster away by using protective amulets, garlic, or objects made of iron. Common parallels suggest the al may have originally been based on the Hebrew Lilith. Some scholars have also suggested a connection with the alu, an evil spirit from Sumerian and Akkadian mythology that was held responsible for nightmares and night terrors.

ALKHA

The Buryat people of Siberia tell stories of a monstrous flying head named Alkha or Arakho. This disembodied head causes solar and lunar eclipses when it attempts to devour the sun or moon. Alkha is most likely humanoid in appearance, as the myth parallels that of Rahu, a decapitated asura in Indian mythology. There are numerous regional variations of the Alkha myth. According to some variants, the Alkha may be an entire class of beings that lurk in the sky.

In some versions of the myth, Alkha had enormous wings with which he would fill the heavens and block the sunlight from the earth. The gods finally chopped him in two, causing his body to fall away, but his head remained in the sky. After this, his head would attempt to devour the sun or moon, yet the sun or moon would simply fall out of him each time he swallowed it.

Following a different interpretation, the Buryats throw stones and make noise during every eclipse in order to save the sun or moon. One myth claims that Alkha gnaws on the moon a little bit each night, making it smaller and smaller as the month progresses, and then vomits it back up, allowing the moon cycle to start over. Sometimes he eats the sun but throws it up quickly due to its heat. Where the monster is known as Arakho, it is said that he used to pursue humans and eat the fur that grew on their bodies. This is why humans are now bare skinned. The gods decapitated him out of disgust, and then his head took to the sky.

ALKONOST

—See *Gamayun.*

BAGIENNIK

The bagiennik is one of several types of mythical beings inhabiting the wetlands of Eastern Europe. Its name means "swamp lurker" in Polish and is also the name of a type of moss. Due to their reclusive nature and underwater habits, bagienniks are seldom seen, and few details of their appearance are known. Sometimes they are described as diminutive humanoids, brownish green in color. They may possibly have reptilian, amphibious, or fish-like qualities. Bagienniks can breathe through their skin by absorbing oxygen in the water. Their presence underwater can be indicated by discolored water and small bubbles rising to the surface. They can be aggressive when protecting their territory, yet their attacks are rarely fatal, and they generally keep to themselves. They are said to serve or worship a being named Wada, or Pani Jezior, Queen of the Underwater Meadow.

The most distinctive characteristic of the bagiennik is its nose. The creature's nostrils are located up on its forehead, like a turtle, allowing it to expose its nose while otherwise remaining submerged. Bagienniks can shoot a burning, oily substance out of their nostrils for self-defense. According to some Polish sources, they can also kill their enemies with toxic breath. Despite its use as a weapon, their nasal oil has amazing medicinal properties. It can be used to treat a wide range of maladies, including fever, indigestion, deep wounds, arthritis, infertility, and heart disease. Their entire skin is thought to be coated with this slime. Contemporary sources often label the bagiennik as a demon. Originally, these beings were probably nature spirits akin to faeries and merfolk.

CHUCHUNAA

The chuchunaa, also spelled *chuchunya* or *tjutjuna*, is a kind of large, fur-covered humanoid from Siberia. Alternative names for this cryptid include mirgydy, meaning "broad shoulders," or mulen, meaning "bandit." It may be continuous with the almas of Mongolia and the yeti of Nepal, although the chuchunaa has certain characteristics that make it distinct. Cryptozoologists classify the chuchunaa as a "marked hominid," due to the fact that some individuals are described as having light-colored patches or markings on their otherwise dark fur. The chuchunaa grows up to 7 feet tall and has long, narrow footprints with splayed toes. Unlike most cryptid hominids, the chuchunaa sometimes wears animal pelts as clothing. It is generally thought to be more human-like than the other ape-like cryptids of the world.

The indigenous Tungus and Yakuts claim to have frequently encountered the chuchunaa in the past. Occasionally, the hominids were blamed for attacking dogs and raiding barns and cabins. The cryptid's supposed existence was taken seriously in the academic world in the early twentieth century. A branch of the Russian Geographic Society conducted an expedition in 1928 to gather more information. They discovered that people sometimes hunted chuchunaa, and thus the hominids were at risk of extinction. In 1933, a Professor P. Dravert urged the Soviet government to recognize the chuchunaa as human beings and grant them legal protection. No such law was ever enacted, however. The British anthropologist Myra Shackley reported observing a chuchunaa in 1985, who was dubbed Mecheny by the Mnasi-speaking locals. Sightings have dramatically dwindled over time, and some cryptozoologists fear that the chuchunaa has gone extinct.

DOUBLE-HEADED EAGLE

The image of an eagle with two heads appears in imperial symbolism throughout Eastern Europe. It has appeared on coats of arms in Russia, Austria, Hungary, Serbia, Germany, and other countries. Its origin in heraldry is often credited to the

Byzantine Empire, which adopted the double-headed eagle sometime around the tenth or eleventh century. The distinctive bird thus became identified with imperial theocratic rule in Eastern and Central Europe. Ivan III of Russia adopted the double-headed eagle as the Russian national emblem in 1497. The symbol was banned from Russia in 1917 but became reinstated in 1993, after the collapse of the Soviet Union. Russian culture identifies the double-headed eagle with strength, unity, and the ongoing battle of good versus evil.

In actuality, the double-headed eagle predates the Byzantine Empire. It is thought by some scholars to be originally based on a Turkic mythical bird called the Oksoko. A sacred being, Oksoko has its roots in an ancient central Asian shamanistic religion called Tengriism. According to this interpretation, the two heads symbolize two different mythical birds named Turul and Konrul. These are divine, benevolent, giant eagles that mediate between Heaven and Earth. Due to its supposed Turkic origin, the Seljuk Empire also adopted the double-headed eagle emblem around the same time as its adoption by the Byzantines. However, it remains unknown how or when the mythical bird first appeared in Turkic symbolism. It may have even-earlier roots in Siberian folklore, India, or the Middle East. Double-headed birds also appear in ancient Assyrian iconography and Hindu mythology.

DREKAVAC

The drekavac of Serbia and Bosnia is a terrifying creature known for its loud, blood-curdling cry. Its name means "the screamer." The description of its appearance is not consistent, yet it typically has some combination of human and dog-like features. Oftentimes it is imagined as ghoulish and emaciated, with a disproportionately large head. It is usually child sized. Some claim it can shapeshift and take the form of a normal-looking animal.

Drekavacs are traditionally said to be the transfigured souls of children who died before being baptized. According to one myth, they were produced when Turkish soldiers forcibly impregnated Serbian women during the Serbian-Ottoman War in the nineteenth century. The drekavac is known as an omen of death. It is said to kill its victims with its voice, or hearing its cry otherwise indicates that someone is dying. It can also kill a person by letting its shadow fall over them. If someone dreams about this monster, it means they will later see one in real life.

Today the drekavac is a bogey used for scaring children. Most adults do not take the myth seriously, although there are exceptions to this. In recent years the creature has become increasingly associated with cryptozoology and paranormal phenomena. Some people allege to have heard its cry at night, and some still believe its cry to be a portent of death. This monster has taken on a role similar to the chupacabras and is sometimes blamed for the deaths of livestock. It is said that drekavacs can be scared away by dogs. They can also be laid to rest by baptizing their formerly human souls.

FIREBIRD

English speakers may immediately think of a phoenix when they hear the name "firebird," but the similarity between these two mythical birds is only superficial. The Russian firebird, or *zhar-ptista*, does not consume itself in flames but instead derives its name from being fire colored and luminous. It resembles a peacock with eyes like jewels. Its marvelous glowing feathers are worth more than gold. Several firebird stories involve a person discovering one of these feathers. Greedy individuals often meet misfortune when they pursue this legendary bird, yet the bird is also known to appear to people in need. Possibly the most famous mythical creature in Russia, the firebird is the subject of a well-known ballet by Sergei Diaghilev and Igor Stravinsky.

One of the most widely known firebird stories is the tale of Prince Ivan and the Gray Wolf. When a czar discovered that the firebird had been raiding his golden apple orchards, he sent his sons out to capture it. His youngest son, Ivan, eventually managed to bring home the bird with the aid of a magical talking wolf. Ivan also acquired other treasures while on his quest, but his two brothers ended up being killed. In another story, the firebird brings light to a kingdom that has been placed under a curse of darkness and deep sleep. The bird bears a handsome prince on its back and wakens a beautiful princess. Later, the firebird carries the princess to a cave belonging to the wicked witch responsible for the curse. The princess kicks over the witch's cauldron and steals a magical jewel, thus breaking the spell and killing the witch.

GAMAYUN

The Gamayun has the head of a beautiful woman and the body of a large bird, usually an imaginary type of bird with colorful plumage. She is one of three similar-looking creatures in Slavic mythology, the other two being called the Alkonost and the Sirin. The Alkonost is the bird of joy and the Sirin is the bird of sorrow. The Gamayun is the bird of wisdom and prophecy. She has the ability to travel between the three worlds: Heaven or *Prav*, the Earth realm or *Yav*, and the dark underworld, *Nav*. Her primary role is to bring celestial knowledge to the Earth realm in the form of song. For example, she delivered the Slavic story of creation to mortals through a series of divine hymns. She may also tell spiritual seekers of their own destiny. The name Gamayun is derived from the Russian word *gam*, meaning speech.

The Gamayun myth originated in pagan times and has been adopted into Christian lore. The Russian poet Alexander Blok wrote a poem around 1917 titled "Gamayun, the Prophetic Bird." Blok's poems were generally apocalyptic in nature. He portrayed the Gamayun as a herald of destruction, with "her lips covered in blood" as she sings about impending horrors. His poem references the violent occupation by the Tatars in Russia that lasted from 1237 to 1462. Another literary work featuring the Gamayun is called *Roza Mira* by Daniil Andreev, written around 1950. This is an esoteric book merging Christian and Buddhist mysticism. Andreev casts the Gamayun as an Archangel in the form of a bird who sang the holy Vedas to early Hindus.

IKU-TURSO

Iku-Turso, or Tursas, is a sea monster of the Far North. He is known from Finland, a country whose language indicates a closer relation to Siberian tribes than to its Germanic neighbors, Sweden and Norway. This beast's appearance is not always agreed upon, although he is frequently thought to be part humanoid, and possibly also part walrus. Some Finns alternatively regard Iku-Turso as being octopus-like, which may reflect influence from the kraken of their Nordic neighbors. To make matters more complicated, Iku-Turso has epithets of "thousand-headed" and "thousand-horned." He has been depicted in numerous ways by various illustrators. In the end, he has essentially become a generic giant sea monster.

Although his appearance is extremely vague, certain details about Iku-Turso are more distinct. For one, he is known to be very ancient. His name means "Eternal Turso." The Finnish national epic, the *Kalevala*, refers to him as the "Son of Old Age." Some scholars speculate that he was once an ancient walrus god and perhaps a god of war. He is sometimes said to be the son of Äijö, the god of the sky and thunder. In other sources he is considered a bringer of disease. Armed with a bow and arrows, the sea monster shoots people to inflict illness upon them.

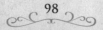

In the *Kalevala*, Iku-Turso was summoned by the dark sorceress, Louhi, who ruled a shadowy northern land called Pohjola. Louhi possessed a magical object called the Sampo and called the sea monster to guard it. Eventually the hero Väinämöinen battled Iku-Turso and sent him back to the bottom of the sea forever.

KARAKONDZHO

According to legend, a large, hairy monster visits southeastern Europe at the onset of each winter. It is called karakondzho or karakondjul in Bulgaria, karakondžula in Serbia, karakoncolos in Turkey, and kallikantzaros in Greece. Krampus of Alpine folklore appears to be continuous with the same myth. The monster is usually described as a grotesque humanoid with horns, hooves, and thick fur.

The karakondzho may have been considered a nature spirit in earlier times. It is said to dwell underground or sleep in wilderness areas throughout most of the year, until it runs amok immediately after the solstice. It is said in parts of Turkey that the creature will ask people questions and then kill them if they answer incorrectly. Yet, in many regions it is thought to be merely mischievous rather than deadly. The karakondzho is active for a ten- or twelve-day period each year, the exact dates differing between countries. These days are generally considered unholy.

Despite this, people in many regions hold a traditional festival during the period of the monster's activity. In Bulgaria, this is a lively carnival called the Kukeri. This involves costumed performers who dance in the street, play fiddles, and act as clowns. Some of their costumes resemble the karakondzho itself. The Christian church has often identified the karakondzho as Satan and, at times, interpreted the Kukeri ceremony as evidence of devil worship. Yet the myth of karakondzho predates any belief in Satan. Rather than worshipping the creature, it is clear where the Kukeri festival is held that the monster's presence is unwanted. The dancers' bells and loud noises are actually intended to drive it away.

KHAIYR MONSTER

In 1964, a team of scientists from Moscow State University was surveying Lake Khaiyr in the Sakha Republic of eastern Siberia. A biologist on the team, Nikolai Gladkikh, reported to the others that he observed a large reptilian creature crawl out of the lake to feed on grass. The other scientists did not believe Gladkikh until they saw the creature for themselves. The animal was black in color, with a long neck, small head, and two small horns. Its most distinctive feature was an elongated dorsal fin running the length of its spine. The team leader, geologist G. Rukosuyev, speculated that it was a prehistoric species. They reported the incident in the Russian newspaper *Komsomolskaya Pravda*. It became one of the most famous lake monster sightings in world history.

Folklore quickly grew over the following years concerning Lake Khaiyr. It became portrayed as a dark and ominous site where birds were afraid to descend on the water, and native Yakuts supposedly told legends of the monster. However, Gladkikh stepped forward in 2007 and confessed that the entire account was fabricated. In fact, he was not even a scientist, but a migrant worker who had been helping with the expedition. Nonetheless, some diehard cryptozoology fans point to the fact that other sightings have also been reported from Lake Khaiyr. Others turn instead toward other lakes in the Sakha region that are rumored to be home to monsters, particularly Lake Labynkyr and Lake Vorota. Despite the alleged sightings, scientists have said these lakes do not contain enough food to support a population of large animals.

KIKIMORA

The kikimoras are tiny female faeries or spirits from Slavic folklore. Historically they have been imagined as looking like frail, homely old women with long, flowing hair, and standing only a few inches tall. Sometimes they are also thought of as invisible spirits or shapeshifters. Yet, the kikimora took on a new appearance in the twentieth century, following a famous drawing by the Russian artist Ivan Bilibin. Bilibin's 1934 illustration depicts the kikimora as a tiny yet nightmarish monster. She wears women's clothing, yet has chicken feet, hairy skin, a beak-like snout, long ears, horns, claws, and beady eyes. For some people this image has replaced the more human-like interpretation of the kikimora.

Although they come from the wilderness, kikimoras are commonly regarded as household spirits. Once they enter a human dwelling, they preside over traditionally feminine domains such as the spinning wheel, the kitchen, and the henhouse. They are reputed to torment people who live in the house, usually children, although they rarely cause any serious harm. However, seeing a kikimora can cause a person to go mad. If a person catches her while she is spinning wool, it is an omen of that person's impending death. Christian tradition has cast the kikimora as demon. Yet in Slavic pagan tradition, the creature was thought to bless people who take good care of their home. Its wrath would only be unleashed if the condition of the home was neglected. In both versions it is nearly impossible to force a kikimora out of a house. One can only prevent a kikimora from entering by burying an object made of silver outside the door.

KOERAKOONLASED

The koerakoonlased, or peninukid, are a race of dog-men from Estonia. Humanoid with the heads of dogs, these bogeys prey on humans, especially children. There are different regional variants of these monsters. In some versions their bodies are divided by right and left, being human on one side and dog-like on the other. Sometimes they have just a single eye in the center of their face. The koerakoonlased is said to be repelled by the toxic berries of the buckthorn shrub, which is traditionally used as a purgative.

A similar monster from Bosnia, Montenegro, and Croatia is called the psoglav or psoglavac, meaning dog head. This human-eating beast has a dog's head, a single eye, the legs of a horse, and iron teeth. It dwells in a land that is rich in gems and jewels, yet is dark like night all the time. This may be an allegorical reference to the Ottoman Empire.

The koerakoonlased and its Balkan counterpart are examples of cynocephalus. Meaning "dog head" in Greek, this term refers broadly to any mythical humanoid with a dog's head. Such beings are referenced in historical writings from various cultures. The cynocephalus has often been used as a metaphor to dehumanize foreign peoples who are perceived as barbaric. Estonians link the koerakoonlased to agents of Ivan the Terrible in the Livonian War, which lasted from 1558 to 1583. The agents were said to wear the skins of dogs' heads on their helmets, symbolizing their role to "sniff out" enemies of the czar. Estonians also applied the term "koerakoonlased" to the Cossacks when they invaded eastern Europe in the 1700s.

LESHII

One of the more prominent creatures from Slavic folklore is a shapeshifting forest spirit called the leshii, or leshy. *Les* means "forest" in Russian. The leshii's true form is generally imagined as humanoid and male, with a long beard and long, wild hair. These beings may be hairy and have other animalistic features, such as horns, hooves, and a tail. They also have tree-like qualities, including green coloration and rough, bark-like skin. Leshiis are capable of changing their size. They may manifest as giants or be only a few inches tall. When people see a leshii, it is usually disguised as a human, or an animal such as a wolf or bear. Similar mythical beings include the woodwose of Western Europe, the basajaun of Basque Country, and the archura of Turkey. All of these creatures are guardians of the forest and protectors of animals.

The leshiis' relationship with humans is ambivalent. They rarely cause serious harm but are reputed to capture women and children who stray close to the woods by themselves. Leshiis are also infamous for playing pranks on unwary travelers. They may raise tree roots to cause them to trip, or switch the places of surrounding objects. Despite their reputation as relentless mischief makers, leshiis are also known to extend acts of kindness when a person has demonstrated their respect for nature. A person can enter a pact with a leshii by resigning from the Christian faith and swearing loyalty to the pagan forest spirit. As tricksters, they also appreciate being told a good joke. Leshiis are afraid of fire and can be driven away with an open flame.

OLGOI KHORKHOI
(MONGOLIAN DEATH WORM)

The most terrifying creature of the Gobi Desert is a venomous burrowing worm called the olgoi khorkhoi in Mongolian. It is also known in Kazakhstan as the büjenzhylan. English-speaking cryptozoologists often refer to it as the Mongolian death worm. Its Mongolian name means "large intestine worm." Red in color, its appearance has been compared to an intestine filled with blood. It is 2–5 feet long and thick bodied like a sausage, with no differentiated head or tail and no eyes. This worm is said to be so toxic that to touch it brings instant death. Anything it comes into contact with corrodes as though burned with acid. It can also shoot deadly venom through the air and is rumored to be able to deliver an electric shock. An entire herd of camels can die by walking over an olgoi khorkhoi buried in the sand.

Many Mongolian nomads believe in the existence of the olgoi khorkhoi. Their belief has attracted cryptozoologists from Russia, the Czech Republic, and the United States. These researchers have never found any physical evidence of the creature, and few people purported to see it live to tell the tale. Some Mongolians attribute the olgoi khorkhoi's deadly venom to the roots of poisonous plants it eats. They refer specifically to the saxaul plant, as well as a parasitic plant called the goyo, which grows on the roots of the saxaul. The creature has a seasonal pattern of behavior, being most likely to appear aboveground in the summertime. Many cryptozoologists feel that the olgoi khorkhoi is a plausible species, but speculate that its deadliness is highly exaggerated.

SEMARGL

Semargl, or Simargl, is a fiery, winged dog in East Slavic mythology. He is often presumed to be a Slavic adaptation of the simurgh from Persian mythology. However, many Slavic pagans believe that Semargl is the older of the two, or that they are altogether unrelated. The Slavic creature is male, whereas the simurgh is female. Sometimes he is depicted as a lion rather than a dog. Some sources cite Semargl as the father of Skif, the mythical founder of Scythia. Christianized sources portray him as a Doomsday hound, chained to the star Polaris to prevent him from devouring the other stars. Pagans describe Semargl as a protector of seeds and grains, especially barley. He is of divine origin and is sometimes considered a god in his own right.

Slavic neopagans associate Semargl with Svarog, the blacksmith god who tends the celestial fire. According to one version of the creation myth, Svarog created the blazing creature in his forge at the beginning of time. Semargl was a shapeshifter made of molten iron. He could take the form of a flying dog, a man on horseback, or a bird of prey. Everywhere he ran he left a charred trail behind him. Svarog sent him to fight against a giant evil serpent, yet he was knocked into the water and defeated. Svarog then repurposed Semargl to become a protector of the fields, hearth, and home. Sometimes he is associated with the household goddess Mokosh. He can also protect people from illness. In Ukrainian folklore, April 14 is Semargl Day. This is when the snow begins to melt due to Semargl's fiery presence.

SHAHMARAN

Shahmaran comes from Kurdish mythology and is also known to the Persians and Tatars but is most prevalent in southeastern Turkey. The creature's name means "king of the snakes," although it is actually a female. Shahmaran, or Şamaran, is described in literature as a large serpent with a woman's head. However, traditional Kurdish artwork gives her a more embellished appearance. At the end of her tail is a second head like that of a snake. Her stout, serpentine body is supported by six or more small feet, which are also shaped like snake heads. She is adorned with ornate jewelry and a crown. Shahmaran dwells in an underground cavern filled with snakes and honey. She is benevolent and known for her great wisdom.

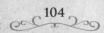

According to legend, a man named Tahmasp (alternatively, Cemshab) once stumbled into Shahmaran's lair. He fell in love with her but eventually returned home. Later, the king fell ill, and his advisor told him that eating the flesh of Shahmaran would cure his illness. The king's soldiers found Tahmasp and tortured him into divulging where Shahmaran lives. Then they went out and captured her. Before they killed her, she told them that anyone who eats her tail will receive uncanny wisdom and whoever eats her head will die. The king's advisor ate her tail and suddenly died. Tahmasp tried to commit suicide by eating a piece of her head, yet he received great wisdom. Shahmaran had tricked them so that her wisdom would be transferred to her lover. Incidentally, snakes have never forgiven humans for killing their noble leader.

SHURALE

Shurale, or Şüräle ("SHUR-a-lay"), is a forest-dwelling monster from the folklore of the Tatars and Bashkirs, two Turkic ethnic groups from central Asia. As a fur-covered humanoid, he is similar to folk monsters from other central Eurasian peoples. Shurale is distinguished from the others by a single horn on his forehead. He also has long, bony fingers with which he can tickle people to death. Parents would often tell their children about Shurale in order to scare them. Any person who falls asleep in the woods may fall prey to this tickling bogeyman. Shurale is the subject of a Russian ballet written by the Tatar composer Farid Yarullin. The titular monster is portrayed as a wicked tyrant who rules over the forest.

The Tatar poet Ğabdulla Tukai wrote a famous fairy tale about Shurale in the early twentieth century. In it, Shurale emerged from the shadows when a young man was splitting a large, heavy log. The monster invited him to play a game of tickle. The woodcutter said he would cooperate if Shurale helped him move the heavy log. Shurale put his hands on the log, immediately getting his long fingers trapped inside the crevice. The monster angrily screamed insults and threats of punishment at the top of his lungs. He demanded to know what the young man's name was. Cleverly, the young man replied that his name was Belter, which means Last Year. Shurale yelled, "My fingers are trapped, Last Year!" All the other forest creatures heard his cries of distress, but they were confused by his words and none of them came to help him.

TULPAR

The national emblem of Kazakhstan depicts a pair of horses with large wings and the horns of gazelles. The Kazakhs are a Turkic ethnic group who, like their neighbors, come from a historical tradition of equestrian nomadism. Scientists believe that all domesticated horses actually came from Kazakhstan originally. The tulpar appears in myths from several central Asian countries, including Kazakhstan, Kyrgyzstan, Uzbekistan, and Mongolia. Representing the perfect horse, it has the wings of a falcon or kite, a bird traditionally considered sacred. The tulpar does not necessarily fly; rather, the wings indicate its uncanny speed and overall auspicious nature. The gazelle horns only appear on the Kazakh version. Some stories connect it to bodies of water as its origin. Today, Kazakhstan has a high-speed domestic train service named the Tulpar.

Different mythical heroes were said to ride on tulpars, including Köroğlu from various Turkic cultures and Manas from the Kyrgyz national epic. In several stories the tulpar is bestowed to the hero at a young age. In some tales it grows up alongside him as his surrogate brother. In the epic of *Manas*, the god Tengri creates numerous tulpars for the hero and his warriors. The animals' wings are usually invisible but will appear in times of extreme distress and darkness. Another epic featuring the tulpar is *Shan Kyzy Dastany*, written in 882 by Mikail Bashtu. The tulpar in this story gained its wings after they fell off a supernatural crow named Kanga. Anyone who rides the horse in eight circles will become the king of the Earth. The tulpar therefore becomes an object coveted by humans and supernatural beings alike.

VAMPIRE

The Serbian word *vampir* refers to a transformed human, usually undead, who preys on mortals by drinking their blood. This description applies to numerous types of demonic beings in Slavic and Romanian folklore. There were many variations of this myth in the Middle Ages. A person can become a vampire if they are bitten by one, but also if they commit evil deeds before death, die in a gruesome manner, become possessed by a demon, or are denied a proper burial. In Ukraine, the *upyr* resembled the modern idea of a vampire but was not necessarily dead. In Romania, the *moroi* is undead, yet mortal, and feeds on people's energy rather than their blood. Other varieties were believed to turn invisible, and some were more like ghosts. Some kinds of vampires had the ability to turn into wolves and were related to werewolves. They did not traditionally turn into bats; this was a later interpretation by Westerners.

Eastern Europeans used to conduct vampire hunts in a similar manner to witch hunts. Nearly any abnormal quality could mark a person as a vampire. Persons suffering from advanced tuberculosis were especially suspected. The disease could cause patients to take on a ghastly pale appearance, with their teeth appearing to grow longer as their gums receded. They would also cough up blood. Vampire hunters used to dig up dead bodies and drive stakes through them or behead them. Vampire folklore entered the English-speaking world in the eighteenth century, becoming popular in the literary trend of Gothic fiction. The Western perception of the vampire is based primarily on Bram Stoker's *Dracula*, published in 1897.

VODYANOI

The vodyanoi are a race of underwater humanoids from Slavic folklore. Vodyanoi is its Russian name, yet it is known by other names in different countries. Between the various countries there are many interpretations of what this race looks like. Typically, vodyanoi are imagined as fish-like humanoids, sometimes as little old men covered with scaly skin and pond slime. They are occasionally envisioned as mermen, while in other regions they look fully human. A 1934 lithograph by the Russian artist Ivan Bilibin depicts the vodyanoi as an anthropomorphic frog-like being with an old man's whiskers. This illustration has influenced many people's perception of the creature's appearance.

These mythical beings probably originated as a type of faerie or nature spirit. They have become perceived as evil demons in recent history. Vodyanoi are infamous for dragging people underwater and drowning them. Many people claim that these beings keep the souls of their victims in jars and use them as slaves.

These creatures reside in luxurious palaces at the bottom of lakes, especially in millponds. People disturb the vodyanoi's habitat every time they build a new mill. The vodyanoi will always claim a human life in retaliation. In some regions it is believed that the millers make pacts with the vodyanoi. The creature then poses a threat to everyone else except the miller. The miller regularly appeases the vodyanoi by sacrificing chickens, or even the occasional wandering drunk. In the Czech Republic and Slovakia, some vodyanoi, or vodnici, are actually friendly. Friendly ones will help fishermen catch fish, especially when offered gifts of tobacco for their pipes.

WEREWOLF

—See chapter four.

YETI

—See chapter eight.

ZMEY GORYNYCH

The Zmey Gorynych, or Slavic dragon, appears to be a cross between a Western European dragon and the Greek hydra. This multiheaded beast is usually depicted with three heads, although in some versions it may have nine heads or more. It is typically envisioned as bipedal with two small front limbs, a stout body, and small wings. Its description is reminiscent of a Persian three-headed serpent called the Aži Dahaka, and it may be derived from the same original myth. In Slavic tales, extra heads on a serpent-like creature typically indicates that it is extremely powerful. Multiheaded serpents appear in various narratives of the Slavic Pagan creation myth. These monstrous reptiles rise up from the sea or the underworld and commit villainous acts, warranting the gods to intervene.

The proper Zmey Gorynych is featured in the tale of the Russian folk hero Dobrynya Nikitich. Dobrynya Nikitich is a legendary *bogatyr*, or knight errant, who had larger-than-life prowess. In his first battle against the Zmey Gorynych, he wielded a holy Christian priest's hat as a weapon. He filled the hat with heavy mud and hurled it up at the dragon, taking off some of its heads. The Zmey Gorynych then begged for mercy and promised to never harm another soul in Russia. It then flew across the border and abducted the princess of Kiev. Dobrynya traveled all the way to Kiev, where he engaged in a grueling battle against the Zmey Gorynych. A voice from Heaven encouraged him to continue fighting and finally instructed him on how to dispose of its body. In the end, Dobrynya freed the princess along with hundreds of other captives.

Chapter Six

NORTH AFRICA AND
THE MIDDLE EAST

This chapter's mythology comes from the arid region stretching from North Africa through western Asia. Despite its seemingly harsh climate, this is the location of the Fertile Crescent, sometimes called the cradle of civilization. During the Bronze Age this area produced some of the earliest large-scale societies in the world. It is also home to some of the world's first written languages and later became the birthplace of Judaism, Christianity, and Islam. Major cultural centers include Egypt in North Africa, Mesopotamia (now Iraq), and the Israel-Palestine region. East of the Fertile Crescent lies Iran, the seat of the Persian Empire. Ancient Persians practiced a religion known as Zoroastrianism, which went on to influence the underlying cosmology of Christianity and Islam.

The mythical creatures in this chapter are Egyptian, Mesopotamian, Hebrew, Persian, and Arabic. The legacy of all these cultures shaped the foundation of Western civilization and the course of world history. Even after other regions developed elaborate civilizations of their own, Middle Eastern and North African cultures continued to influence their achievements. The earliest great scholars, philosophers, scientists, and mathematicians of the Arab world appeared centuries before the European Renaissance. Their scholarship provided necessary groundwork for the scientific discoveries of the West. Among these contributions was the Arabic numeral system, which is now used all around the world.

AMMUT

Ammut, or Ammit or Amermait, is known as the Devourer of the Dead or the Eater of Souls in Egyptian mythology. This beast is part crocodile, part lion, and part hippopotamus. These three species were considered to be the most aggressive animals in Egypt. Ammut is a female despite being depicted with a mane like a male lion. Occasionally she is portrayed as being part leopard instead of part lion. She was as feared by ancient Egyptians as all of her comprising animals would suggest. Despite this, she was also a sacred being and an enforcer of divine law. Sometimes she is described as a goddess in modern books, although this is not technically correct. The Egyptians did not worship Ammut; she was essentially a pet that belonged to the gods.

Ammut serves a critical role in the judgment of the dead in the ancient Egyptian religion. When a person died, the Egyptians believed that the god Anubis brought their soul to a sacred place called the Hall of Double Justice. There, the dead person testified to the gods that they were virtuous in life. After their testimony, the gods weighed the person's heart on a scale against the Feather of Truth. The Egyptians believed that the heart contained the soul. If the person was wicked and their heart was laden with sin, it would be heavier than the Feather of Truth. When this was the case, the heart was fed to Ammut, thus ending the person's existence. The Egyptians referred to this as dying a second time. Fortunately, most souls passed the judgment process.

ANZU

Anzu is an ancient Mesopotamian mythical creature sometimes described as a "reverse griffin." He was frequently portrayed as an enormous eagle with the head of a lion. Some images depict him as a winged quadruped with the forelegs of a lion and the hind legs of an eagle, the opposite of a standard griffin. This creature is thought to have originated in the early civilization of Sumer, where he was a personification of stormy weather. His name originally meant "eagle," yet the Sumerians described the ferocious storm spirit as having sharp teeth and roaring like a lion. Anzu was born on Mount Sharshar, where his birth suddenly unleashed powerful winds, dust storms, and raging water. There was also a constellation of Anzu in ancient Mesopotamian astronomy.

Anzu has been portrayed both positively and negatively in mythology. This creature befriended the titular hero in the Sumerian legend *Epic of Lugalbanda*. Lugalbanda discovered Anzu's nest and took care of the juvenile chick. In return, Anzu graced Lugalbanda with preternatural strength and speed, which the hero would need for his later exploits.

It is also thought by some scholars that Anzu may have once been regarded as the protector of the sacred Tablet of Destinies, which belonged to the god of wisdom, Enlil. Yet, according to Akkadian myth, Anzu looked upon the Tablet of Destinies and immediately became possessed with greed. The creature then stole the sacred tablet and thus acquired extraordinary power. The gods sent out a hero from their ranks, either Ninurta or Marduk, depending on the version, who defeated Anzu in an epic battle.

BEHEMOTH

According to the ancient Hebrews, Behemoth is the largest and most powerful animal on land. This enigmatic beast is described in the Book of Job. As God touts His power to Job, He reminds Job that He created this colossal beast. The context is to teach Job humility and instill him with fear, not of the creature itself but of the one who created it. God compares Behemoth's bones to brass and iron. It has the ability to drink up an entire river. The creature cannot be killed or subdued by any being other than God. Jewish folklore states that Behemoth dominates the land as Leviathan dominates the sea, and as a giant bird called the Ziz dominates the sky. There are various speculations that God will destroy Behemoth at the end of time or that Behemoth will fight the Leviathan at the end of time.

Many religious people believe Behemoth is a real animal, although they do not agree on what kind. One may logically think it is an elephant, the largest animal on land. Yet the ancient Hebrews were probably unfamiliar with elephants. A hippopotamus is a more likely candidate, as the Hebrews could have seen those in Egypt. However,

Behemoth's tail is said to move "like a cedar," implying that it is heavy and powerful. The tail is not a prominent feature on either elephants or hippos. Young Earth creationists favor the theory that Behemoth is a type of dinosaur, a sauropod such as Brachiosaurus. Others believe that Behemoth is simply a metaphor for God's power and is not a real animal.

BURAQ

Al Buraq, or *al-Borak*, is a miraculous horse-like being from Islamic belief. Its name means "lightning" or "shining one." Eastern Persian artwork is responsible for its designation as a mythical creature, depicting it as a horse with colorful wings, a woman's head, and a peacock's tail. The gender of this animal is ambiguous. Although it is shown with a woman's head, Muslims often regard it as male. Al Buraq is widely known from these embellished images, yet these are not universal to all Islam and are not taken literally by all Muslims. Al Buraq is not specified to have a human face in any Islamic holy text but is described as a "beautiful-faced creature." Essentially, al Buraq is the angelic version of a horse. It comes from a section of Heaven called the Paradise of Buraqs, which is populated by forty million of these creatures.

Al Buraq appears in the Quran as the holy steed of the angel Gabriel. Gabriel lent al Buraq to the prophet Mohammed to begin his amazing Night's Journey. In the first part of this journey, called the Isra, al Buraq took the prophet from Mecca to "the farthest mosque." Many Muslims interpret this as Masjid-Al-Aqsa in Jerusalem. On the second part of the journey, called the Mi'raj, al Buraq brought Mohammed up on a tour of Heaven. There he received mentorship from the earlier prophets, including Abraham, Moses, John the Baptist, and Jesus. Also during this journey, Mohammed stopped and tied al Buraq to the holy Western Wall in Jerusalem. Today, Muslims refer to this wall as the Al-Buraq Wall.

DIV

A race of evil beings from Persian myth, the divs are often labeled as demons in English. The Persians historically believed in a variety of evil beings, the divs being only one kind. These monstrous humanoids are large and dim witted, with animalistic features such as claws, tail, and horns. Their skin may be hairy or spotted, the latter being reminiscent of disease. Sometimes these monsters are blamed for causing physical and mental illnesses in humans. The word *dīv* ("deev") is derived from *daeva*, meaning "false god" in Avestan. They are most likely the product of Zoroastrians demonizing gods from India, which are called devas and are actually benevolent.

Divs are often portrayed as foolish and easy to outwit. For instance, they tend to do the opposite of whatever they are told. They may also leave themselves vulnerable by sleeping for days at a time. They also have an external soul that they keep in a jar, or inside another object or animal, which can potentially be destroyed by a hero.

Numerous divs appeared in the medieval epic narrative called the *Shahmaneh*, by Ferdowsi. One prominent villain was the White Div, or Div-e Sepid. This was the chieftain of the divs in the land of Mazandaran, where he captured a king and his soldiers and held them in a dungeon. The great hero Rustam killed the White Div and freed the prisoners. The king and his men had gone blind in the dungeon, but Rustam used the div's blood as medicine to restore their sight. Rustam would later defeat another powerful div named Akvan in a different adventure.

GIRTABLULLU

Girtablullu is the name of a half-human, half-scorpion species that appears in iconography from various ancient Mesopotamian civilizations. The creature is bipedal with a human head. Below the neck can be any combination of human and scorpion parts, depending on the example. A large scorpion tail is always present. Many later depictions also give the girtablullu wings and the feet of a bird. Its human head usually sports a beard and a headdress associated with divinity. Despite their variety, archeologists refer to all of these forms as girtablullu, or "scorpion men." The earliest

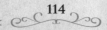

known example is from Ur at around 2500 BCE. These creatures became more prevalent in the later civilizations, especially Assyria after 900 BCE. They sometimes appeared on cylinder stamps and seals belonging to the wealthy elite.

In the *Enuma Elish*, the girtablullu was one of the monsters produced by Tiamat to battle against Marduk and the other gods. Marduk captured the girtablullu and the other monsters and repurposed them to serve beneficent deities. Later depictions of the girtablullu portray it in a religious context, with its arms raised as though praising the sun god Shamash, or with a human worshipper standing before it. This has led some archeologists to speculate that the girtablullu worked as a herald of Shamash or another god. The creature also served an apotropaic role, meaning that its image was believed to ward away illness and other evil forces. Neo-Assyrian exorcists used to recommend burying a male-female pair of girtablullu figurines, along with effigies of other mythical beings, to protect palace and temple gates.

HUMA

The legendary huma, or homa, is a heavenly bird from Iran. Whenever this bird casts a shadow on a mortal, their soul is essentially being touched by Heaven and they are blessed with good fortune for the rest of their life. If the huma alights upon a person's head, the person is blessed with kingship. This bird also remains perpetually in flight, never coming to rest. In some cases it is imagined as lacking feet. The huma's appearance was never described in literature, as the bird is essentially invisible. Occasionally it is said to be both male and female simultaneously.

The huma appears in the medieval Sufi fable *The Conference of the Birds*, by Farid un-Din Attar. In this story, the huma attends the gathering of all feathered fowl, who embark upon a journey in search of the king of the birds. The huma decides not to participate in the quest, as its duty in granting kingship and fortune to humans is too important to abandon its post.

Over time, the huma became conflated with other mythical birds, such as the phoenix, the simurgh, and the griffin. An ancient statue of the huma exists in Persepolis, Iran, the former capital of the Persian Empire. This statue resembles a griffin, possessing a bird's beak as well as mammalian ears and paws. The huma is sometimes referred to as the Bird of Paradise and has found its way into Western travelers' tales under this name. Westerners named real birds from Indonesia and the South Pacific after this legendary species. Yet, ancient Persians who first imagined the huma would have never seen these birds.

HUMBABA

Humbaba, or Huwawa, is an ogre from the *Epic of Gilgamesh* in ancient Mesopotamia. His job, as assigned by the god Enlil, was to kill any human who dared to enter the Cedar Forest. Personifying the natural elements, Humbaba could summon the powers of fire and floods with his roar. This roar was referred to as the *abūbu* weapon. He could also kill with his breath and was protected by seven mystical auras. Humbaba is generally envisioned as a giant humanoid. His face is hideously wrinkled like coiled intestines. Beyond this, the details of his appearance are vague and highly variable. Sometimes he is portrayed as having horns, and occasionally paws and other animalistic features. Gilgamesh's savage-born companion, Enkidu, is often depicted as looking similar.

The great hero Gilgamesh was determined to kill Humbaba. Assisted by the sun god Utu (Shamash), Gilgamesh succeeded in mortally wounding the forest guardian. Once defeated, Humbaba bargained for his life. He sought comradery with Enkidu, whom he recognized as wild-born. Humbaba begged Enkidu to persuade Gilgamesh to spare him. He renounced his allegiance to the god Enlil, swearing loyalty to Gilgamesh instead. He even offered to give up his forest to him. But Enkidu urged his friend to finish his foe. Humbaba then cursed Enkidu to die before Gilgamesh. Gilgamesh went ahead and killed Humbaba, thus granting Mesopotamians access to the timbers of the Cedar Forest. Later on, Enkidu fell ill and died, just as Humbaba had wished upon him. Gilgamesh was so disheartened by the loss of his best friend that he sought a medicine that could cure death. He never succeeded in finding it.

KARKADANN

Regarded by Westerners as the Persian unicorn, the karkadann is thought to be the evolutionary predecessor of the European icon. Yet, in several sources from the Middle East it is clear that the karkadann is a distinct species unto itself, one that is larger and far more frightening than its European cousin. The medieval scholar Abu Rayhan al-Biruni described the karkadann as being built like a buffalo, black in color, with thick scaly skin, a single curved horn, and three yellow hoof-toes on each foot. Today it is understood that al-Biruni was actually describing the Indian rhinoceros. But few if any medieval Persians had ever seen a rhinoceros. The Persians produced numerous fanciful variants of the mysterious karkadann, some more closely resembling the Western unicorn, and others resembling one-horned versions of bulls and other animals.

The karkadann is regarded as extremely dangerous. It is so territorial that it poses a threat to any animal it can see or smell. Usually it is said to feed only on vegetation, yet occasionally it is considered predatory. All animals flee from the karkadann except for the ringdove, whose sweet song can pacify the ferocious beast. Sindbad the Sailor reported from his second voyage that a karkadann killed an elephant by impaling it on its horn. It is nearly impossible for a human being to kill a karkadann. Normally, the only way to obtain its horn, which has medicinal properties, is to find the creature already dead. The legendary hero Isfandiyār managed to kill two of the animals but was only able to accomplish this feat because he possessed divine armor that made him invincible.

LAMASHTU

The female monster named Lamashtu is possibly the most evil being from Babylonian (Mesopotamian) mythology. She is humanoid-shaped with a lion's head, donkey ears, and eagle talons. Her body is covered with fur. Oftentimes she is portrayed with her clawed hands raised at her sides, dripping with blood. She is often depicted suckling animals from her breasts, variously including dogs, pigs, and snakes. Sometimes she appears standing on a donkey's back.

Lamashtu was a wind spirit. She was originally born among the gods, her father being the great sky god Anu. Once her evil nature became known, she fell from grace and was cast down to the underworld. Her bestial form is reflective of this nature. The Babylonians generally portrayed evil spirits as animalistic and the true gods as human-like. Lamashtu resembled a race of wind and storm spirits called the ugallu, although most of these beings were male. All wind spirits in Babylonian mythology were malevolent, capable of spreading disease and death. Lamashtu was the worst of all. Virtually all images of this monster are plaques and amulets intended to ward her off.

Lamashtu could attack any person, yet her favorite victims were newborn babies and women in childbirth. She was known to steal newborn babies and eat them. It was believed that she would appear above a pregnant woman or a woman who was giving birth. To deliver a fatal curse, she would touch the woman's belly with her claws seven times. This could result in a stillbirth or miscarriage. Only a being named Pazuzu was able to keep her away, although he was not always successful.

LAMASSU

The lamassu, or aladlammû, is a majestic sphinx-like beast from the Assyrian and Babylonian civilizations of ancient Iraq (Mesopotamia). The name *shedu* is also associated with this species. This creature takes the form of a winged bull with a human head. It is often portrayed alongside the winged, lion-bodied Babylonian sphinx. Wingless versions also exist, as do rare upright, humanoid forms of the lamassu. The winged quadrupedal bull form is the most common. The creature's bull body shows thick, curly hair on its breast, back, and flanks, indicating that it is an extinct aurochs or possibly a bison. The human head of this creature displays a long, well-groomed beard, an ornate headdress, and large earrings. Some scholars speculate that the bull-bodied lamassu was sacred to the storm god Adad, while its lion-bodied counterpart was sacred to the goddess Ishtar.

There are many representations of lamassus in Mesopotamian art. They were especially popular in the Kassite kingdom, which lasted from 1531 to 1155 BCE in Babylonia. The most famous representations were pairs of monumental statues that would flank the entrances to temples and palaces. The statues are actually built with five legs rather than four. The lamassu was not literally a five-legged animal; the statues were designed that way to create an optical illusion. From the front, the beasts appear to be standing at attention with their legs planted solidly beneath them. From the side they appear to be walking. Ancient artists rendered them this way to convey the impression of power and authority. Mesopotamians also depicted the lamassu on talismans and in other contexts to ward away evil forces.

LEVIATHAN

Leviathan is known from Hebrew texts as the most powerful and dreadful creature of the deep. Its name means twisted or coiled in Hebrew, suggesting it has a writhing, serpentine shape. According to the book of Job, Leviathan has terrifying teeth and armored skin composed of scales tightly sealed together. The creature is seemingly a fire-breather or has a source of burning flame inside its head. Smoke billows from its nostrils, sparks leap forth from its gaping mouth, and its eyes shine like the rising sun. It has the ability to heat up the water and make the ocean boil. No mortal can kill this creature. Some Christians later came to identify Leviathan with Satan, as an enemy of God. However, Psalm 104 mentions Leviathan as simply another sea creature that God created.

An additional detail about Leviathan is provided in medieval Jewish texts of the Midrash and in the comments of Rabbi Shlomo Itzhaki. These sources state that God initially created two of these colossal serpents. He then decided that their species posed too great a danger to the world if they were to breed. For the safety of the world, He dispatched the female and served up her flesh at an exclusive banquet of the righteous. The male Leviathan survives today as the only representative of his kind. In Isaiah 27:1, it is said that God will destroy this creature at the end of days. It is possible that the ancient Hebrews imagined this beast after stumbling across prehistoric fossils. Some Young Earth Creationists believe the monster to be a surviving prehistoric species such as Mosasaurus or Zeuglodon.

MANTICORE

—See chapter three.

MI'RAJ

The al-mi'raj, or simply mi'raj, is a little-known mythical animal from Islamic literature. Described in medieval Islamic poems and bestiaries, the little beast is a yellow rabbit with a horn on its head. This horn is black, spiraled, and remarkably long. This and other horned rabbits of world mythology may have been inspired by a real-life phenomenon. In rare cases, a form of Shope papilloma virus has been known to cause rabbits to develop horn-like growths on their skin. The word *mi'raj* means ladder in Arabic, possibly referring to the mythical creature's upward-pointing horn. This is not to be confused with the more common usage of the word, referring to the prophet Mohammed's ascent into Heaven, as the horned rabbit is anything but heavenly.

The al-mi'raj is larger than a normal rabbit, perhaps the size of a dog, yet not an enormous beast. Nonetheless, with its 2-foot-long horn and its alarming vigor, it is able to kill humans and animals far larger than itself by stabbing them repeatedly. It will attack its victims both out of territoriality and for food. This unlikely carnivore is able to devour surprisingly large amounts of meat at a time. Other animals immediately run away when they see it. Iskandar, a fabled version of Alexander the Great, reportedly saw one on the mythical island of Jezîrat al-Tennyn in the Indian Ocean. The people on this island fear the mi'raj for the threat it poses to themselves and their livestock. They sometimes resort to hiring witches to ward the creature away. Fortunately for people elsewhere, the mi'raj does not live anywhere else besides that island.

MUSHUSSU

The mysterious mushussu of Babylon is best known from images on the walls of Ishtar Gate. The creature appears on this monument alongside lions and wild bulls to protect the Mesopotamian city. The mushussu is a composite of various animals yet is nonetheless graceful-looking. It has four long legs, a snake's head and neck, and a body covered in scales. Its front feet are paws while its hind feet resemble eagle talons. It has a thin tail raised upward like a cat. On its head are two tall horns and a pair of curly plumes, which may be its ears. The mushussu's name, formerly mistranslated as sirrush, means "fierce snake" or "red snake." Its species was birthed by the primordial monster-mother, Tiamat. Initially an enemy of the gods, the creature was later repurposed by the god Marduk after he defeated Tiamat's army.

Around 1800–1750 BCE, King Hammurabi installed Marduk as Babylon's chief deity and the mushussu as a symbol of Marduk. The creature was often depicted alongside the warrior god, lying at his feet like a dog. An inscription by King Neriglissar mentions seven mushussus made of copper that protect Babylon by spraying its enemies with deadly venom. In addition to Marduk, the mushussu was also associated with Nabu, the god of wisdom and writing. Some tablets depict the mythical creature seated before a worshipper, bearing on its back a stylus and a spear. These are the symbols of Nabu and Marduk, respectively. Some scholars have also suggested a connection between the mushussu and the storm god Adad, who was also considered a protector of the city.

PAZUZU

Pazuzu is a monstrous supernatural being from Babylonia and Assyria in Mesopotamia. He has four wings, hands and feet like eagle talons, a face like a mastiff, and a tail like a scorpion. He is always depicted with his right hand raised and his left hand lowered, which archeologists refer to as "smiting pose." Modern sources frequently label Pazuzu as a demon. This word is misleading, however, as it recasts this ancient Babylonian figure in Christian terms.

Pazuzu was actually a powerful nature spirit controlling winds. Indeed, he was dangerous and had a wrathful disposition. The Babylonians and Assyrians did not romanticize nature but instead saw it as a chaotic force that was at odds with human progress. They blamed the wind for the destruction of crops and the spread of disease. Wind spirits were considered malevolent, and Pazuzu's winds were the most powerful of all. Some ancient sources claim Pazuzu controlled the scorching southwestern winds from the Arabian Desert. Other sources identify him with the frigid northeastern winds from the Zagros Mountains. In both versions of the myth, Pazuzu had the ability to crush the winds that came from other directions.

The fact that he could block other winds, which were also considered evil, means he had beneficent qualities in addition to dangerous ones. Many people believed he would protect them from other malicious beings if they honored and appeased him. In particular, he alone could fight off the deadly spirit Lamashtu, who often came to harm babies and pregnant women. Women sometimes wore amulets of Pazuzu's likeness or kept them in the house for protection.

PHOENIX

The brightly colored, everlasting phoenix bird is one of the most widely known mythical creatures in the world. Its origin appears to be a complicated blending of myths from various places. Some scholars trace it to the *benu* from ancient Egypt, a divine heron that symbolized immortality. Yet, the proper phoenix as it is recognized today is distinguished by the cycle of being consumed in flames and reborn from the ashes. This characteristic is not mentioned in any Egyptian texts; neither is it associated with any East Asian bird that Westerners identify as a phoenix.

Instead, the earliest references to this bird may come from Hebrew texts. In the Tanakh, Job says, "I shall die with my nest, and I shall multiply my days as the phoenix"

(Job 29:18). In a Jewish legend the phoenix was named Milcham and it lived in the Garden of Eden. It was the only creature that did not eat the forbidden apple after Eve shared it with the other animals. God then separated it from the other animals by building a wall around it, where it now enjoys a life span of 1,000 years. It expires naturally and then is burned in a pyre of frankincense and myrrh. God granted it immortality by allowing it to be perpetually reborn after it dies.

According to the Jewish apocalyptic texts, the phoenix dwells in the Third Heaven. On its wings are golden Hebrew letters that read "Neither earth nor Heaven bring me forth, but wings of fire bring me forth." It flies alongside the sun as it moves through the sky, using its wings to shield the earth from being burnt.

ROC

Possibly the world's most famous mythical giant bird, the roc or rukh comes from Arabic folklore. Its appearance is described as being similar to an eagle or vulture, yet one of unbelievable proportions. The bird is so enormous that it blocks out the sun when it takes to the air. Some Renaissance travelers purported that it was a real bird.

The Moroccan explorer Ibn Battuta allegedly sighted a roc on his travels to the China Seas in the 1300s. The Venetian explorer Marco Polo claimed that a feather from a roc measured twelve paces long and was used for pooling water.

The most-famous stories about the roc are those associated with the fictional character Sindbad the Sailor. While on his second voyage, Sindbad found himself stranded on a desert island with a roc's nest. Sindbad escaped from the island by tying himself to the sleeping roc's ankle with his turban cloth. When the roc awoke it carried him to a faraway valley filled with diamonds. There, he witnessed rocs preying on giant serpents that could swallow elephants, and on a karkadann that had an elephant impaled on its horn.

Later, on his fifth voyage, Sindbad's crew foolishly opened a roc's egg and cooked the chick for dinner. Shocked and alarmed, Sindbad urged his men to vacate the island immediately. They sailed off, but the adult rocs pursued their ship, carrying massive boulders in their talons. Before long, the colossal birds caught up with them and dropped the boulders on the ship, smashing it to pieces. Sindbad then became shipwrecked, which led him directly to his next fantastic misadventure.

SEDJA

Also known as a serpopard, the sedja resembles a cross between a serpent and a leopard. The creature is a large feline similar to a lioness, but with a long serpentine or swan-like neck. Very little is known about it, although the images depicting it are extremely ancient. Sedjas appear on various artifacts from Old Kingdom Egypt, between 3000 and 2000 BCE. The same species also occurs on Middle Eastern artifacts from around the same time period or slightly earlier, in Uruk in Mesopotamia, and Elam in what is now Iran. The name *sedja* means "one who traveled from afar" in ancient Egyptian. It is often depicted in pairs, the two animals facing each other with their necks intertwined. Some scholars interpret the circle created by the animals' necks as a solar symbol. One famous example of this image appears on an Egyptian artifact called the Narmer Palette. This palette shows the sedjas being tethered by humans with ropes as though they are domesticated.

Archeologists had at one time identified the sedja with the Egyptian goddess Mafdet, due to its appearance on Egyptian tombs. Mafdet assumes the shape of a feline and protects people from serpents. This explanation is no longer popular. Another theory is that the sedja may have once been a conceptual representation of a giraffe, depicted by an artist who had never seen an actual giraffe. This hypothesis is tenuous as well. Sedjas continued to endure in Egyptian art into the Middle Kingdom, well after giraffes became better known and were portrayed as a separate species. Sedjas were also depicted alongside other mythical creatures.

SETH'S ANIMAL

The Egyptian god of chaos, Seth (pronounced "Set"), is depicted with the head of a strange animal. The creature's ears have square corners as though they have been cut. Its downward-pointing lips resemble those of a grazing herbivore. Historians used to assume it was a real species but could not agree on what kind. Only after finding images of it shown in full body did they realize Seth's animal is a mythical creature. It has a canine or feline body and a straight tail resembling an arrow. Its Egyptian name has been listed variously as *sha*, *shu*, or *hiw*. Little is known about this mysterious beast, yet some clues can be inferred from myths about Seth and the hieroglyphics associated with the creature.

The god Seth is infamous for having murdered his brother, Osiris, who was the benevolent king of the gods. Seth chopped Osiris's body into pieces and scattered them across the land. He served a brief and brutal reign before losing a battle against Horus, the son of Osiris. Where Seth's animal is referenced in hieroglyphics, it is sometimes represented with the image of a chopping tool. This same hieroglyph also means "to separate." Other hieroglyphics depict the animal with a knife on its head or back. The word *hiw*, one of its possible names, indicates something loud and belligerent. Seth himself is said to have a loud, thunderous voice, as he is associated with storms. The Greeks identified Seth with the chaotic monster Typhon; for although the two do not look alike, they were thought to serve a similar role in mythology.

SHADHAVAR

The shadhavar is a Persian mythical beast related to the unicorn and the karkadann. It resembles a gazelle or antelope, although it is larger and taller than the natural species and has a distinctly different horn. Its single horn is large and hollow, filled with forty-two branching chambers that end in holes. When the creature raises its head to the wind, the air blows through the horn and produces a melody like a flute. One folkloric account states that a king was once gifted a shadhavar's horn. The wind blew through it as he held it in his hands, producing a melody most beautiful. Yet the music had a supernatural quality. People around the king became enraptured by the sound, filled with bliss, as though by hypnosis. Then, when the king turned the horn upside down, the tune became profoundly sad. The people became possessed with grief and were compelled to weep.

Medieval Persians believed the shadhavar to be a real animal. It was featured in *The Wonders of Creation*, a lengthy bestiary by the thirteenth-century scholar Zakarīyā ibn Muhammad al-Qazwīnī. In this book, the shadhavar is depicted as looking sheep-like, light brown in color, with a very large horn. Yet despite its appearance as a shy herbivore, the shadhavar is actually a fierce predator. This trait is consistent with other single-horned animals in Persian mythology. To catch its prey, the shadhavar raises its head up high and catches a breeze with its horn. This carries its hypnotic tune across the land. Humans and animals flock toward the source, entranced. The shadhavar then swiftly kills and devours them.

SHAHMARAN

—See chapter five.

SIMURGH

The simurgh or senmurv of Persia has seen a long evolution with many different incarnations and mythical influences. This complex creature apparently originated as a mystical bird known as the saena, which is mentioned in the Zoroastrian holy text called the *Avesta*. The early simurgh or saena was described as a gigantic female bird of prey. She lived atop the Tree of All Seeds, also known as the Tree of Life or Tree of Knowledge. The seeds would fall to the earth whenever she would beat her wings. Some texts claimed the saena would suckle her young like a mammal. Later, the simurgh or senmurv would be depicted with the head of a dog and became the symbol of the Sassanian Royal Empire. Islamic folklore conflated it with the phoenix and once again portrayed the simurgh as fully avian. It appears as the king of the birds and a symbol of enlightenment in Sufism, a mystical school within Islam.

The simurgh plays a role in the Iranian national epic, the *Shahnameh*, or "Book of Kings." This was written by the Persian poet Ferdowsi around 1000 CE. The simurgh rescued a child named Zal, who had been abandoned in the wilderness. She raised him and educated him in language, philosophy, and medicine. Zal later had a son named Rustam, who grew into a great hero. When Rustam was once almost killed by an adversary, Zal called upon the simurgh to save him. Rustam himself later called upon the simurgh to aid his wife in childbirth. In both instances, the simurgh demonstrated prophetic knowledge as well as the ability to heal people's injuries.

SPHINX, EGYPTIAN

The sphinx is the most iconic mythical creature of ancient Egypt. Usually portrayed as a lion with a human head, this concept was used to represent different gods and pharaohs. Some sphinxes bear the heads of animals other than humans, such as falcons, rams, or even Seth's animal. The different heads may represent gods such as Horus, Ra, or Amon. In the late period of Egypt, from around 660 BCE onward, Egyptians began worshipping a protective sphinx-god named Tutu. This being is depicted as a human-headed sphinx striding or standing with alertness, rather than in repose like most sphinxes. Some later depictions show Tutu as having wings, indicating Greek or Roman artistic influence. Traditional Egyptian sphinxes were always wingless.

By far the most famous Egyptian sphinx is the colossal statue known as the Great Sphinx, located on the Giza Plateau. Its face is believed to represent Pharaoh Khafra, who is credited with building it around 2500 BCE. One faction of scholars argues that the monument was actually built 11,000 years ago by a civilization forgotten by time. While mainstream archeologists reject this theory, all agree that the significance and symbolism of the monument have changed over time. Even the Egyptians themselves once forgot its original importance, as they allowed the blowing desert sand to bury the statue up to its neck. Around 1400 BCE, a prince named Thutmose dreamed that the buried Great Sphinx was a god named Horemakhet, "Horus of the Horizon." The sphinx told him to restore it to its original glory and then he would inherit the kingdom. The prince excavated the statue and was later crowned Pharaoh Thutmose IV.

SUHURMASU (CAPRICORN)

Originating in Sumer, Mesopotamia, the suhurmasu is half goat and half fish. Its name is derived from the words meaning carp and goat. It was a symbol of Enki, the god of water and wisdom. To a lesser extent it was also associated with the hero god Marduk. Like many other mythical creatures of Mesopotamia, the image of the suhurmasu served apotropaic purposes, meaning it was used to ward off evil forces. It was also believed to bring in the good. The suhurmasu was sometimes depicted on temples alongside images of mermen called kulullu. But unlike many other Mesopotamian mythical creatures, it was not originally created by Tiamat as an enemy of the gods. Instead it was thought to be a natural animal, at least in the earlier period. Ancient Sumerians may have imagined the suhurmasu after hearing stories about seals and sea lions from faraway lands.

Myths of the suhurmasu did not die out with the passing of Sumerian civilization. Instead, the creature has endured for thousands of years. Babylonians identified it with a constellation in the night sky. Eventually the region was conquered by Alexander the Great, and Babylonian astrology became appropriated as the Western zodiac. Suhurmasu is now referred to as Capricorn. Folklore of this creature thus remains alive today through the tradition of astrology. Capricorn is sometimes identified simply as a goat and other times a "sea goat." This zodiac sign is associated with hard work and ambition. Persons born under this sign are said to be determined, practical, and stubborn, with great leadership skills. In relationships they are said to be faithful and committed.

TIAMAT

Tiamat is a being embodying primordial chaos in the ancient Babylonian and Assyrian creation myth called the *Enuma Elish*. Also referred to as Mother Hubur, Tiamat is a great watery monster whose essence is that of a deep, churning sea. She existed at the beginning of time, accompanied by a male counterpart named Apsu, who represented fresh water. Tiamat's appearance is never actually described in the ancient myth. Modern scholars usually presume her to be serpentine or dragon-like.

Tiamat gave birth to numerous primordial serpents and monstrous beings. Her favorite son was named Kingu, and Apsu's favorite son was named Mummu. Her other offspring went on to produce the gods, who resembled humans in their appearance. One day, Apsu and Mummu acted against Tiamat's wishes and waged war against the gods. The gods destroyed them. Tiamat then decided to avenge her husband and son. She mated with Kingu in order to produce an army of serpents and monsters. She placed Kingu at the head of the army and gave him the Tablet of Destinies to wear as armor.

Yet, the warrior god Marduk slew Kingu and would later create humans from his blood. He also seized the Tablet of Destinies, which would allow people to have society and laws. Then Marduk killed Tiamat and ripped her in half. Separating the halves, he designated one as the sky and the other as the earth. Afterward, Marduk built the first ziggurat upon the earth. This act immortalized his triumph and laid the foundation of civilization. This creation myth establishes the Mesopotamian worldview that humankind is righteous and destined to trump the chaotic forces of nature.

Chapter Seven

SUB-SAHARAN AFRICA

Home to some forty-eight countries, Africa is the second-largest continent in the world. The six northernmost countries constitute North Africa, which are culturally more similar to the Middle East. The rest comprise sub-Saharan Africa. Sub-Saharan Africa was the birthplace of humankind around 300,000 years ago. To this day there is more genetic diversity in Africa than on any other continent. Rich in culture, sub-Saharan Africa is home to around 2,000 indigenous languages. It has supported numerous flourishing kingdoms and empires, including Aksum, the Nok, the Songhai, the Oyo, the Mutapa, and many others. Most of Africa's contemporary social problems stem from colonization and the slave trade.

Mythical creatures from sub-Saharan Africa tend to be grossly underrepresented, if not altogether absent, from most books about mythology. This has nothing to do with an absence of mythology in Africa, but instead with the Western world's general lack of familiarity with African culture. Most indigenous African folklore is passed down through oral tradition and is not recorded in print. Only limited information is accessible to non-Africans, which has mostly been collected by Western colonials and cryptozoologists. Therefore, numerous African mythical creatures are presented as "cryptids" in the West. Books frequently portray these creatures as potential new species waiting to be discovered, rather than products of creative minds and cultural lore. Unfortunately, there is relatively little literature describing the actual African perspective on their own monsters.

ANANSI

Anansi, or Kwaku Ananse, is one of the most well known and endearing of African mythical beings. The word *ananse* means spider in the Akan language of West Africa. The mythical character is both a spider and a human. He is sometimes considered a shapeshifter and other times imagined as a creature with combined human and arachnid features. Non-African sources often label Anansi as a god. This is most likely due to his close relationship with the supreme sky god, Nyame or Nyankopon. This creator is often said to be Anansi's father and is sometimes also called Ananse Kokuroko. Yet, the Akan state that Anansi himself was human and they do not worship him. According to some regional interpretations, Anansi began as a human being, and Nyame turned him into a spider or spider-man as a punishment for being so mischievous.

Anansi originated among the Ashanti people, a large subgroup of the Akan. This culture has an incredibly rich oral tradition. Anansi is almost synonymous with Ashanti storytelling, as he is the keeper of all the stories. Folk stories are referred to as *Anansesem*, or "spider stories." These tales, which contain all the wisdom of the culture, once belonged to Nyame rather than Anansi. They were at that time called *Anyankosem*, "God's stories." Nyame would not give these stories away to anyone unless they paid a seemingly impossible price. Anansi used trickery to fulfill the god's demands and thus became the owner of all the stories. The "spider stories" remain popular as children's entertainment, even today. They are even popular outside Africa, especially in Jamaica.

DINGONEK

The earliest known written account of the dingonek comes from 1910, in Edgar Beecher Bronson's book *In Closed Territory*. Bronson details the experience of John Alfred Jordan, a big-game hunter who purportedly saw a strange beast in the Maggori River in Kenya. Jordan repeatedly compared the monster's appearance to a big cat but also called it a reptile. He said it looked like a hodgepodge of leopard, sea serpent, and whale. It was spotted like a leopard, 12–18 feet long, armored with large, plate-like scales, and sporting a distinctive pair of saber teeth. Upon seeing it, his Kipsigis trail guides cried "Dingonek!" and fled in terror. A round from Jordan's .303-caliber rifle only glanced off the beast's armored hide.

Jordan was not able to kill the dingonek, yet he claimed that specimens had been killed by other hunters. Although no physical remains survive as evidence, there were a few other Western colonials, British and German, who reported seeing similar creatures. Colonial administrator C. W. Hobley took these stories seriously. Yet, despite Hobley's open-mindedness, most people considered the dingonek to be merely a tall tale. Jordan's account implies that the Kipsigis people, and possibly other indigenous Africans, were already familiar with the dingonek. However, it seems likely that this is a myth of Europeans in Africa and may not be based on an indigenous belief at all. A probable origin for the dingonek is the campfire stories of Western big-game hunters. The creature represents the ultimate trophy, the ultimate prize, which is elusive and difficult to kill.

ELOKO

The eloko, or biloko in plural, is a malicious race of dwarf humanoids known to the Nkundo people in Zaire. The eloko's appearance is distinguished by its tiny size and the growth of grass on its head and body in place of hair. This race wears leaves as clothing, dwells inside hollow trees, and spends most of the time camouflaged to the point of invisibility. The biloko were originally human beings but, having been consumed by jealousy and greed, were reincarnated as monsters after their death. They haunt the deepest, darkest part of the forest. There they guard precious fruits and game animals, waiting to kill and eat anyone who tries to collect these foods. They also carry magical bells with which they place spells on their victims. These little monsters are able to open their giant mouths wide enough to swallow people whole.

A common eloko story tells of a woman who accompanied her husband into the deep forest. The man emphatically warned his wife that if she heard the sound of bells outside their hut, she must not answer or else she will die. While he was gone, the woman heard the bells and became mesmerized. Soon she saw the eloko, who looked innocent and helpless. The pitiful creature said it was starving, so she let it inside. The woman was completely bewitched. She permitted the hungry eloko to cut out pieces of her flesh with a knife and eat them. The hunter returned to the hut and killed the eloko with his spear. However, it was too late for his wife, who soon died.

EMELA-NTOUKA

The emela-ntouka is a monstrous beast from the folklore of Central Africa. It is said to dwell in the Likouala Swamp in the Congo and the Democratic Republic of Congo (DRC), in the Dilolo swamps of Angola and Zambia, and in various surrounding regions. This gigantic creature is an herbivore yet is highly aggressive and capable of killing any other animal. It is especially infamous for its ability to kill elephants. Its weapon is a single massive horn made of ivory, which grows from its snout.

The name *emela-ntouka* comes from the Bomitaba tribe in the Congo. Most sources state that it means "killer of elephants," although it could also mean "water elephant." Other names from other languages include chipekwe, ngamba-namae, and aseka-moke. Some groups of people conflate it with the mokele-mbembe. The emela-ntouka has an elephant-like body, head, and ears. It is said to be approximately the same size as an elephant and has similar skin. Yet, unlike an elephant, it has no trunk, and its tail is long and thick like a crocodile's. Its distinctive white horn may grow up to 5 feet long. The emela-ntouka is also said to produce a loud bellow or roar. It spends most of its time in water.

This legendary beast caught the attention of Western big-game hunters in the early part of the twentieth century, and of cryptozoologists more recently. Cryptozoology enthusiasts have suggested that it may be either an unknown type of rhinoceros or a living dinosaur. Unfortunately, Westerners pursuing this creature have tended to only focus on its physical description instead of African narrative tales about it.

GA-GORIB

Ga-Gorib is a villainous monster from Khoi folklore in the Cape of southern Africa. This being is the subject of one of their most well-known legends. According to some sources, the monster's name is a bastardization of *Gai-Gaib*, meaning "the thrower down." Others point out that *Gorib* means "the spotted one" in the Khoisan language, a common epithet for leopards and other spotted animals. Aside from this possible clue, the KhoiKhoi people do not provide any detailed description of the monster's appearance. He is usually assumed to be a large grotesque humanoid like a type of ogre. He also has thick, rubbery skin.

Ga-Gorib guards a large pit surrounded by rocks, where he sits at the edge all day long. When people pass by, he taunts them into throwing rocks at him. The rocks bounce back off his thick skin and strike the thrower, causing the person to fall into the pit. Eventually a man named Heitsi-Eibib decided to put an end to the monster's reign of havoc. Heitsi-Eibib was no ordinary man, but a legendary hunter with magical powers. The hero resisted Ga-Gorib's insults and jeers until the monster grew tired of taunting and looked away. As soon as Ga-Gorib turned his head, Heitsi-Eibib was able to land a rock right behind his ear. This was his one vulnerable spot. In another version of the story, Heitsi-Eibib fought the giant ogre by wrestling him. All versions of the legend end with Ga-Gorib toppling into his own pit. Some add that Heitsi-Eibib even sealed the pit shut afterward, ensuring that the monster would never climb out.

GROOTSLANG

The name "grootslang" means "giant snake" in Afrikaans. Afrikaans is a postcolonial language derived primarily from Dutch, and therefore grootslang is not an indigenous word. The name designates a category of mythical creature, referring to any monstrous African snake. In fact, gigantic snakes are perhaps the most ubiquitous mythical creature in Africa. Only in South Africa do the locals refer to legendary giant snakes as grootslang, although similar serpents appear in folklore throughout much of the continent. In some myths, these serpents are said to be the product of a snake mating with an elephant; hence their enormous size.

The proper grootslang of South Africa is a blending of indigenous and colonial folklore. The serpent is 40 to 50 feet long and 3 feet wide and has diamonds for eyes. The South African grootslang is said to inhabit a deep cave in a rugged wilderness region called the Richtersveld. The cave itself is legendary, as it reputedly houses a massive trove of diamonds. It is known as the Wonder Hole and the Bottomless Pit. The grootslang protects this fabled treasure, which is probably as fictional as the snake. It is said that nobody who enters the cave comes back out.

This legend is fueled by the expedition of Peter Grayson, who left England in search of the Richtersveld diamonds in 1917. He had been accompanied by six other men, yet misfortune befell their mission. Two men died, one fell ill, another was injured, and the other two deserted before they ever reached the cave. Grayson himself never returned, and the locals know he was devoured by the grootslang.

IMPUNDULU

The Zulu and Xhosa of South Africa speak of a magical "lightning bird" called the impundulu. This bird materializes as a flash of lightning, which is the only way most people can see it. Its true appearance is imagined differently in different regions. In some localities people identify it as a type of stork called the hammerkop, while in others it is a type of hawk. Some say it is black and white; others say it is colorful and fat. Only women can see it in its avian form. The impundulu used to be considered a nature spirit, yet in more recent times it has become associated with evil sorcery. It is thought to assume a human form and will serve witches as their lover and familiar. It has even been blamed for the spread of tuberculosis.

Wherever lightning strikes, the impundulu has laid its eggs. If the eggs are laid near a village, it is imperative that they are not allowed to hatch, as the bird can bring great devastation. In some regions, a shaman must be sent out to destroy the eggs. The Xhosa allege that the surest way to circumvent disaster is to stand in wait with a club for lightning to strike, and then kill the bird as it manifests. In KwaZulu-Natal, shamans are believed to hunt impundulus by luring them with a bowl of fermented milk mixed with special medicine. The bird is then harvested for its fat, which has many medicinal properties, and its meat, which can be made into a magic potion. This potion can allow people to track thieves, or, when misused, control people's minds.

INKANYAMBA

The Zulu and Xhosa traditionally believe that the lake of Howick Falls in South Africa is inhabited by Inkanyamba, an enormous water serpent. Inkanyamba is sometimes described as having a horse-like head. It may also be depicted with a fish's tail and jagged fins along its back. This being is capable of taking to the air. It is responsible for the dramatic storms of summertime, which is thought to be its mating season. The Xhosa attribute lightning bolts to this creature, due to their snake-like shape. Houses with metal roofs may be struck by lightning because the airborne serpent dives down at the reflective surfaces, mistaking them for water. Tornadoes also are seen as manifestations of Inkanyamba's serpentine form. These are exceptionally rare in South Africa, yet a tornado did occur in 1998, making international news. All the locals were talking about Inkanyamba afterward.

The indigenous people treat Inkanyamba with reverence due to his great power. They exercise extreme caution around Howick Falls. Ideally only shamans, called *sangomas*, should be allowed near the lake, and only for the purpose of prayer. Some say Inkanyamba or similar creatures also inhabit other lakes in the forested areas of South Africa. Most Westerners do not understand the religious significance of these water spirits. In the Western mind, Inkanyamba is merely South Africa's equivalent of the Loch Ness monster, which is how it is frequently publicized. Cryptozoology enthusiasts sometimes speculate that the creature is a kind of large eel. Some of the more adventurous ones classify it alongside certain other African mythical animals that they imagine to be living dinosaurs.

ISITWALANGCENGCE

One of the many dreadful creatures of Zulu myth is the isitwalangcengce, meaning "basket bearer." This predator resembles a giant hyena except for its peculiar head, which is shaped like a basket, with its ears appearing as the handles. Its mouth stretches the width of the basket's base, armed with sharp teeth and bone-crushing jaws. Much like the Zulu women who carry baskets on their heads, the isitwalangcengce uses its head to transport food. Sometimes these voracious beasts will enter villages during community meat-sharing. This is when village women go door to door, dropping pieces of meat into each other's baskets. The isitwalangcengce will crouch down near the doorways of houses, pretending to be an ordinary basket. There it catches pieces of meat and then runs off to the wilderness before it can be caught.

Occasionally an isitwalangcengce will become brazen enough to prey on humans. Parents warn their children that if they misbehave, the basket monster will scoop them up and carry them away. Then the isitwalangcengce will throw them down onto a pile of rocks, shattering their skull so it can eat their brains. Fortunately, there is a way to outsmart the isitwalangcengce. If a child is being carried in the creature's head, they should break off sticks from the trees and bushes that are within reach. They may be able to amass a large pile of sticks and jump out before the beast reaches the rocks. The isitwalangcengce will only know that its head is still full and will continue running. If this happens enough times, the creature will completely bury its skull-cracking rocks beneath the branches.

KHOLOMODUMO

Known infamously as the Swallowing Monster, Kholomodumo is from the Sotho (Basotho) people in Southern Africa. Other variants of its name include Khodumodumo and Kammapa. The Sotho do not provide any specific description of its appearance aside from noting its extraordinary size. Their northern neighbors, the Tswana, consider the monster a titanic lizard and call it Kgogomodumo. The Swallowing Monster is said to have existed at the beginning of time. It was enormous from the start, and it continued to grow larger and larger as it swallowed every person and every animal it saw. It traveled the land, devouring everything in its path.

Eventually it grew so large that it could not pass between the mountains and thus became confined to a valley.

One woman in the valley outsmarted the monster. She smeared herself with ashes to conceal her scent and then sat motionlessly, pretending to be a stone. Kholomodumo lumbered right past her and ate everyone else. Not long afterward, the woman gave birth to a boy. This child was no ordinary child, but a magical hero destined to slay the monster. He was born holding two spears and wearing special charms called *ditaola*. From these charms came his name, Ditaolane. In other versions he was called Moshanyana. This young hero grew into a man over the course of one day and bravely set off to kill Kholomodumo. Ditaolane used his superior speed and agility to cut the monster open, without being eaten. He freed all the people and animals that were trapped inside its belly. The people then rebuilt their society and made Ditaolane their chief.

KIKIYAON

The kikiyaon is perhaps one of the world's most sinister mythical creatures. This flying monster is said by the Bambara people to dwell in the forests of West Africa, particularly Senegal and the Gambia. Not all descriptions of it are identical, but this being is typically described as having a humanoid-shaped body and an owl's head. It has arms as well as wings, with talons on its hands and additional claws on its wings. Its beak is armed with sharp teeth. Sometimes it is said to be covered with greenish hair instead of feathers. It also has a vile stench. The kikiyaon can make a sound like an owl, or a different sound like a person slowly being strangled. This chilling call can carry across long distances. Some people claim to have heard this cry, which has allegedly never been identified with any known animal.

Kikiyaon means "soul cannibal" in the Bambara language. This terrifying creature dwells in the supernatural realm and is conjured into the physical world by an evil sorcerer. It can run as well as fly and will utilize both methods to hunt down its victims. The kikiyaon moves very quickly and can travel between worlds. In the dream world it is just as predatory as in the physical world, yet it is unable to smell its prey. For this reason, people who are dreaming have a greater chance of escape. But if they are killed by it in the dream world, their real-world selves are also in grave danger. It is also said that people who hear its cry will become stricken with a deadly illness.

KISHI

"Kishi" broadly means spirit or supernatural being in many southern Bantu languages. As a specific mythical creature, it refers to a being with a dual nature: both human and animal. The kishis' true nature is that of a hyena, which is ravenous for human flesh. Their human aspect is merely a disguise. The kishis appear as handsome, well-dressed men, yet on the back of their head is a second face, that of a hyena. They keep this face concealed behind a headcloth or long hair until they are ready to consume their victims. When a kishi reveals his true form, his head rotates 180 degrees so that his hyena face is in front. He then drops down on all fours and devours his victim alive. These monsters may also have other powers such as shapeshifting, and the ability to cause rain and lightning.

Everything kishis do is a clever trick to kill people and eat them. Their favorite victims are beautiful young women. There are many stories about kishis from various ethnic groups. Some of these stories involve young women being tricked by the predators, who appear to be charming young men. Sometimes the women disobey the norms of their village by travelling far away without a man to protect them. In one story, it is the young women's father who is fooled. Unable to find husbands for his daughters due to a social stigma placed upon him, the father is finally relieved when a pair of well-dressed suitors show up at his doorstep. In some of the stories the women are able to escape from the kishis, yet oftentimes they are not.

KONGAMATO

A flying monster, the kongamato is a relatively famous cryptid from Central Africa. The Kaonde-speaking people of northwestern Zambia describe it as resembling a large lizard with leathery wings like a bat. It is red in color, with a beak or snout filled with sharp teeth. Its wingspan is about 4–7 feet. The name kongamato means "overwhelmer of boats." It is reputed to swoop down at people rowing in the Jiundu swamps, causing their boats to capsize. It kills its victims and then only eats their toes and earlobes. Everyone who sees it dies. The evil power of the kongamato can also cause floods. This myth thus serves to explain the occurrence of floods and drownings. While traveling on the swamp, the locals may utter a magical chant, "*Muchi wa kongamato,*" which offers protection from the creature.

Written information about the kongamato was first published in Frank Melland's 1923 ethnography, *In Witch-Bound Africa*. At that time, Westerners were circulating rumors that Africa harbors dragons and dinosaurs. Melland showed his Kaonde-speaking informants a picture of a prehistoric pterodactyl, and not knowing otherwise, they all agreed it was a kongamato. However, they were not certain on some of the details, since no one had ever seen the creature and lived. Despite this very significant problem, some cryptozoology enthusiasts have accepted their recognition of the pterodactyl as proof that pterosaurs still live in Africa. This interpretation has become especially popular among Young Earth Creationists and is perpetuated in numerous books and websites. This theory constitutes a new Western mythology of the kongamato and should not be confused with the authentic Kaonde myth.

MBULU

The mbulu is one of numerous menacing beings from Zulu folklore in South Africa. The creature is roughly humanoid in shape, although it does not naturally look human. It is an amphibious being covered with scaly skin. It has a long, snake-like tail with a large mouth at the end. This mouth has a mind of its own and is always hungry. The mbulu possesses magical powers. It can take on the appearance of human beings simply by wearing their clothes. It frequently follows people around and whispers in their ears. This altered form is merely an illusion rather than a true change of shape. Its hungry tail is still present while in disguise, even though humans do not notice it.

In one folktale, the mbulu stole a girl's clothes and disguised itself as a woman. This "woman" married a man and kept the girl as her slave. While toiling in the field, the girl sang a disheartened song about what had happened to her. Another woman overheard the song and devised a plan to catch the mbulu. The woman dug a hole in the ground and filled it with milk. Then she held a recreational event, inviting everyone who walked by to jump over the hole. The entire village quickly became involved in the jovial affair. When the mbulu jumped over the hole, its tail immediately dove into the hole to drink the milk. The village suddenly saw the mbulu for what it was, and killed it. The girl was then freed from slavery and she married the man who had mistakenly married the mbulu.

MNGWA

—See *Nunda*.

MOKELE-MBEMBE

The famous mokele-mbembe is said to resemble a sauropod dinosaur such as Apatosaurus. Cryptozoologists have searched for evidence of this creature but sometimes lump different myths together. In actuality it is not always clear that the various accounts describe the same animal. The mokele-mbembe is generally distinguished by its long neck and small head, although in some regions it is seemingly interchangeable with the emela-ntouka. Sometimes it is also said to have a horn, a large single tooth, or a frill like a cockscomb. These characteristics are frequently disregarded in sources that actively promote the dinosaur interpretation. Incidentally, Westerners have had fantasies of dinosaurs living in Africa since the nineteenth century, and this may be creating bias.

Much of what has been written about the mokele-mbembe was recorded by cryptozoologists and focuses on its purported behavior, rather than on folktales. The creature is said to spend most of its time in the water. Its name comes from the Lingala language, meaning "one who stops the river." It is an herbivore but will kill anyone who goes near it. Members of the Bangombe tribe claimed their people once killed one of these animals at Lake Tele in the Republic of the Congo. Everyone who ate its flesh died afterward, supposedly because of its supernatural power. It is also said that a person who sees the mokele-mbembe and then talks about it will suffer a premature death. Despite this, some Central Africans have shown a willingness to talk to Westerners about it once cryptozoologists began showing them pictures of dinosaurs. This outside influence is probably causing their folklore to change.

NANABOLELE

The fearsome nanabolele comes from the Sotho or Basotho culture in Lesotho and South Africa. These large, human-eating beasts are characterized by the light they give off, which is compared to the light of the moon in the night sky. Their appearance is not otherwise described, although it is mentioned that they live in herds. The nanabolele dwell in a mystical underworld located beneath the surface of the water. English-language sources often refer to these monsters as dragons, yet this appears to be a projection by Westerners. In actuality, the nanabolele is a mythical creature unique to the Basotho and is not a dragon per se.

In one Sotho fairy tale, there were two sons of a late chief who were about to be initiated into manhood. Being orphans, their sister, Thakane, served as their caretaker. The boys demanded that their ceremonial clothing and shields be made from the glowing hide of a nanabolele. This was an absurd request, but they insisted that their father would have been able to do it.

Thakane rallied together the bravest hunters in the village and set out to find the nanabolele. They reached a distant river and entered the underworld. There they found the giant beasts and managed to kill one of them as it slept. The other nanabolele were furious at this, yet Thakane and her companions were able to escape with the use of a magic pebble. The beasts pursued them back to the surface world until the village's guard dogs forced them to turn around. In the end, Thakane was able to use the nanabolele's skin to make the shields and clothing for her brothers.

NANDI BEAR

One of Africa's most famous cryptids, the Nandi Bear is associated with the British colonial occupation of Kenya, which lasted from 1888 to 1962. A Geoffrey Williams claimed to have observed a mysterious bear-like animal sometime around 1905 in the homeland of the Nandi tribe. Bears never existed in Kenya, or anywhere in Africa, other than a now-extinct population in Morocco. Yet, a rash of sightings similar to Williams's began around 1912. In actuality, these sightings were not consistent with one another, nor were the animals usually thought to be bears. Rather, "Nandi Bear" became a catch-all term for any animal the colonials could not identify. Various descriptions point to hyenas, baboons, honey badgers, and even aardvarks. Yet, many British colonials believed that the Nandi Bear was some kind of large carnivorous mammal that had yet to be scientifically described.

Soon the colonials began probing the indigenous people for more information about this supposed beast. This was when they learned of various terrifying mythical creatures with names such as geteit, chemosit, and shivuverre. The locals blamed these different monsters for disappearances of cattle at night, and even for unexplained human deaths. The geteit, for instance, is a giant ape-like creature with large claws that cracks open people's skulls and eats their brains. The British colonials assumed that all of these monsters actually referred to the same species and were all the Nandi Bear. Many colonials therefore believed that the Nandi Bear kills people and eats their brains. Nandi Bear sightings seem to have ended by 1960, coinciding with the end of Kenya's colonial period.

NINKI-NANKA

The West African ninki-nanka is a thriving myth in modern day. Although numerous people claim to have seen the strange aquatic reptile, there is much disagreement on what it looks like. Cryptozoologists visited the Gambia in 2006 to collect information, only to discover how complex and varied the creature is. Many sightings are probably of ordinary animals such as crocodiles, pythons, or even dolphins. Others reports are distinctly fanciful. Oftentimes the ninki-nanka is described as serpentine, although some reports claim it has legs. It may live in the swamps or in the sea. It may have horse-like qualities or it may not. Sometimes it has wings, horns, or other distinctive features. But the most frequently occurring traits are an elongated body, shiny reflective scales, and a crest on its head. It is also always large in size.

Many West Africans take the ninki-nanka seriously. The creature is commonly said to bring death to those who see it, usually within a few weeks. Despite this, numerous individuals claim to have seen it and did not die. In the Gambia, the crest of the ninki-nanka is said to bear an inscription of Islamic verses, as most Gambians are Muslim. Anyone who reads the verses will die. However, the creature is not specifically tied to Islam, and the original folklore of its existence may predate the introduction of Islam into the area. Today, outside cultural influence appears to be shaping the ninki-nanka. France and England colonized different parts of West Africa, and European dragons may be contributing to the creature's description. Some people even allege that the monster is fire-breathing.

NUNDA

A Swahili folktale from Tanzania describes a bloodthirsty feline called the Nunda. Its name is derived from the words *mu-ngwa*, meaning "strange one," and therefore it is also called the Mngwa. According to the fairy tale, the Nunda originated as a pet cat belonging to a sultan named Majnun. Allowed to roam free, the cat began growing in size and killing livestock. Sultan Majnun always defended his pet when herders complained of its behavior. Before long, however, the Nunda began to prey on humans. Majnun remained unsympathetic until the cat killed three of his own sons. After this, he declared the beast to be a demon. Soldiers set out to kill it but they always lost their lives. Eventually it was Majnun's own youngest son who succeeded in bringing down the Nunda.

The folktale is fiction, yet there have been people who believed the Nunda is real. This cat was blamed for a string of unsettling deaths in the 1920s and 1930s. Victims were found horribly mutilated, partially eaten. The culprit was described as an enormous feline, gray in color and striped like a tabby. It was said to be as large as a lion but different from any known species. Matted clumps of brindled gray fur were found on some of the victims, yet there was no way at that time to run a genetic test. British colonials investigated the case. They initially chastised the locals for believing in the mythical Nunda. But eventually some Westerners began to wonder if there really was an unknown species of big cat. New species or not, there has not been any sign of the beast in recent years.

NYAMINYAMI

Nyaminyami is the supernatural guardian of the Zambezi River and Lake Kariba between Zambia and Zimbabwe. This land is home to the Tonga people. Nyaminyami is described as having a snake-like body and fish's head. He has gills like a fish, large fangs like a viper, small fins at his sides, and a long, coiled tail. His length is unknown but his body is said to be up to 10 feet wide. He also has a wife who lives under an enormous rock in the lake. This rock is called Kariwa, which means trap. Nyaminyami usually keeps to himself, yet he dislikes people going near the rock. There he creates whirlpools and causes boats to sink. If angered, he is capable of generating devastating storms and floods.

Nyaminyami's wrath was unleashed several times in the 1950s, when British colonials began working on the construction of a dam in the Zambezi River. This massive dam would separate Nyaminyami from his wife. The Tonga warned the Westerners of grave consequences if they were to upset the river guardian. The British disregarded these warnings, and sure enough, devastation ensued. A series of massive cyclones produced epic floods over the course of the decade. Construction of the dam was halted several times, and much equipment was lost. Eighty workers lost their lives in the disastrous storms, the likes of which had never been seen before or since. The dam was finally completed in December 1958. Some Tonga today wear amulets of Nyaminyami for protection. They say the river spirit still causes tremors in the area, and one day he may rise up again.

POPOBAWA

Popobawa is a modern-day monster from Zanzibar, an island state belonging to Tanzania. This terrible creature resembles a gigantic bat with a single eye like a cyclops. Its name means "bat wing" in Swahili. This creature is a sexual predator that targets mostly men. There are people today who not only believe in its existence but claim to have been attacked by it. A rash of traumatizing encounters was reported in 1965 on Pemba, the smaller of the two islands of Zanzibar. The mass hysteria eventually ceased, yet Popobawa has returned sporadically over the years. Another outbreak took place in 1995. Reports have spread through Zanzibar and Tanzania and continue today. In actuality, the victims are probably suffering from a physiological phenomenon known as sleep paralysis. This disorder is held responsible for various myths of night demons around the world.

Popobawa disguises himself as a man during the daytime. At night he can take the form of a cloud of mist or puff of smoke in order to enter a house through a sealed window. Victims may hear the creature's talons scraping on the windows outside before he enters. He also has a vile stench. Survivors are forced to endure further humiliation by telling everyone they know about the attack. If they do not follow through with this order, Popobawa will return to assault them again, even more brutally than before. It is rumored that Popobawa began as an evil djinn or genie that was released by a sorcerer. It is said that Popobawa will only attack people who sleep indoors. He can be thwarted by smearing one's body with pig oil.

SASABONSAM

Sasabonsam is feared by residents of Ghana, the Ivory Coast, and Togo. He is a human-eating bogey who is often used to scare children. The name "Sasabonsam" is translated as "devil" in the Akan language. However, folklore of this monster probably predates the introduction of Christianity and the belief in the devil.

Sasabonsam's appearance is described differently in different areas. In one version he is hairy and red. In another, he is tall and thin with blazing red eyes. In some, he has metal fangs and metal hooks for feet. Sometimes he is given animalistic features, and occasionally, leathery wings. He is often said to hide up in trees and kill people who pass unwittingly beneath him. According to an Akan subgroup called the Sefwi, Sasabonsam is a grotesque giant with eyes like balls of fire, teeth like burning spears, and hair that reaches down to his knees. He also wears a belt with a hammer strapped to it.

Sasabonsam once tormented a particular hunter in a Sefwi folktale. Whenever the hunter would shoot an antelope, he was forced to cut off the animal's legs, and the monster would eat the rest. One day, the hunter's pregnant wife decided to follow him and see why he kept bringing home only legs. The wife saw Sasabonsam and immediately fainted. Sasabonsam prepared to eat the woman, but then the baby emerged from her womb. The baby suddenly grew into a giant and fought against Sasabonsam. Finally, he snatched the monster's magic hammer and killed him with it. After that, he promptly shrank back down and became a baby again. This was the legendary hero named Akokoaa Kwasi Gyinamoa.

TIKOLOSHE

The tikoloshe, or tokoloshe, is an infamous monster species from the Zulu, Xhosa, and Sotho peoples of South Africa. These are tiny, ape-like humanoids covered with black hair. Standing less than 2 feet tall, these creatures are nonetheless extremely dangerous. They are intelligent and capable of speech but always speak with a lisp. They also have magic powers. Tikoloshes carry a magical marble or pebble that allows them to be invisible most of the time. They can also cause disease. At night, tikoloshes may enter people's houses to assault women or bite off victims' toes while they sleep. People can prevent an attack by placing bricks beneath the legs of their bed. If a tikoloshe terrorizes a home or village, people must consult a shaman to get rid of it.

Many Bantu speakers in South Africa believe in the existence of tikoloshes, even today. These creatures are closely associated with the belief in witchcraft. Witches send their tikoloshe familiars out to steal from people and commit other misdeeds. Occasionally, serial murderers are said to have a tikoloshe in their service, which carries out their dirty work for them. It is often thought that these monsters are created by witches. This part of the myth is a more modern interpretation, as the belief in witchcraft dramatically increased over the twentieth century. In earlier times, tikoloshes were regarded as being more like wild animals. They were still considered dangerous, like lions and leopards, but not evil per se. Today, some people imagine tikoloshes as dwelling in lakes and rivers, their original habitat.

WATERLORD

The Fulani, an ethnic group from the West African desert, tell a story of a magical seven-headed serpent that once guarded the people's access to water. The Waterlord held great power over the Fulani. He demanded that they leave offerings for him if they wanted any water at all.

One day, two women were collecting water from the river. One of them tormented the other and filled up her jar with mud. The woman whose jar was filled became very upset and begged the Waterlord for help. The Waterlord answered her call and cleaned her jar but demanded a favor in return. He required that the woman's first-born daughter would become his wife once she came of age. The woman had no choice but to oblige. Eventually the woman gave birth to a daughter and named her Jinde Sirinde.

Not surprisingly, the daughter did not want to marry the giant snake and found herself a human lover instead. Yet, her mother knew she must keep her promise, and she sent Jinde to the river. There, the Waterlord pulled Jinde down to live in his realm. Jinde begged the Waterlord to allow her one last visit to her mother. The serpent agreed to give her one day and one day only. He would come for her at sunset if she did not return. Jinde tried to go back to her parents, yet they would not let her in. Then she went to see her boyfriend. Before she knew it, the sun was setting and the Waterlord was right behind her. Her boyfriend came out with a sword and cut off all seven of the Waterlord's heads.

Chapter Eight
SOUTH ASIA

This chapter combines two extraordinary regions, South Asia and Southeast Asia. The giant that is India dominates this region and its mythology. The cultural richness and historical achievements of India are far too elaborate to convey here. India is the world's second-largest nation in terms of population and is expected to surpass China as the largest in the next few years. India is also a cornucopia of religious diversity, being the birthplace of Hinduism, Buddhism, Jainism, and Sikhism. Other South Asian countries include Indonesia, which has the world's fourth-largest population, as well as Thailand, Sri Lanka, Nepal, Bangladesh, Malaysia, and others. South Asia gave rise to a number of sophisticated civilizations in ancient times, with many scientific achievements predating those of the West.

India's mythical literature easily exceeds that of ancient Greece. Indian mythology is intertwined with belief systems still widely practiced today. The word "myth" is not considered a dismissive term in South Asia as it is in Western religion. Many South Asians regard their myths as important allegories containing great wisdom, not as fairy tales. Most creatures in this chapter are sacred beings held dearly by hundreds of millions of persons of faith. Some of them are gods transformed into animalistic beings. Others are holy creatures that serve the gods or otherwise appear in ancient religious stories. There are also evil monsters, yet these are less common.

AIRAVATA

Airavata is a great celestial elephant. In India he is portrayed variously as having five heads, or one head with seven trunks and four tusks. In some representations he looks like a normal elephant, although white in color. Sometimes he has wings. In Thai mythology he is called Erawan and is said to have thirty-three heads. Each of these heads has seven tusks, and each tusk is many millions of feet long. Within each tusk resides thousands of celestial beings and seven lotus ponds. For the sake of simplicity, this elephant is usually only depicted with three heads in Thai and other Southeast Asian art. The three-headed Erawan appeared on the flag of Laos from 1893 to 1975.

In all accounts, Airavata is the largest and mightiest elephant in the universe. He is also the *vahana*, or mount, of the god Indra. Considered the most powerful of the Vedic gods in ancient times, Indra is the god of war and storms. Airavata is likewise associated with rain and clouds. He produces the rain by drawing up the cosmic water with his trunk and spraying it over the earth.

According to the *Mahabharata*, Airavata came into being when the gods were churning the great Ocean of Milk. In another myth, the god Brahma created sixteen cosmic elephants to guard the eight directions of the universe. Airavata was the first of these and is assigned to the direction of east. East is the portal of Heaven and is guarded by Indra. Airavata is paired with a female elephant named Abharamu. The gods and elephants ruling each direction are called the Lokapalas or Dikpalas.

ASHVAMUKHI

The word *ashvamukhi* means "horse face" in Sanskrit. Various horse-faced beings exist in Hindu myth, with one class referring to a type of yakshini. Yakshinis are magical female forest beings, similar to the nymphs in Greek mythology. Most yakshinis are beautiful vixens, yet the ashvamukhi is a terrifying horse-faced variety. It is also a deadly predator.

One tale of the ashvamukhi concerns a queen who lived in the city of Varanasi. This queen was unfaithful to her husband, the king, prompting him to accuse her of betrayal. The queen refuted the accusation. She insisted that if she was guilty, she may be reincarnated as a yakshini with a horse's head. The queen was reborn in her next life as an ashvamukhi, exactly as she had said.

Having a horse head, she was not able to seduce men with her looks like the other yakshinis. Instead she resorted to evil ways, taking men by force and devouring them. She also left the forest to live in the desert, perhaps because the other yakshinis did not want her among them, and she made her dwelling in a cave. One day the ashvamukhi abducted a traveling Brahmin. She was going to kill him, yet she fell in love with him instead. She held him prisoner in her cave and had a son with him. She loved this son dearly. Eventually the Brahmin escaped and took the son with him, never to return. The ashvamukhi died of a broken heart. This incident fulfilled her karmic debt, and she could be human again in the following life.

BARONG

Barong is a mythical creature from Bali, an Indonesian island known for its distinctive culture. The spirit of this sacred, magical beast inhabits an ornate wooden mask. During the ceremonial Barong Dance, a pair of performers don a full costume of the four-legged Barong. The costume is elaborately decorated with long, shaggy fur, shining gold plates, an upright tail, and bells. The mask is kept in a temple when not in use. Barong is defined by his role rather than his appearance. Different regions of Bali have their own local Barong masks, each inspired by different kinds of animals. The most famous is the Barong Singa or Lion-Barong, from the region of Gianyar. Despite its name, it looks little like an actual lion. Other regional Barong masks are based on the tiger, wild boar, dog, deer, buffalo, and serpent.

The Balinese believe Barong is a real being, the king of the supernatural spirits. The performance associated with this being is both entertaining and religious. Barong battles a nemesis named Calon Arang, who is also portrayed by a masked dancer. Calon Arang bewitches the other performers, and Barong must break the spell to save them. Barong's heroism enforces the concept of dharma, or cosmic order. All of the costumed dancers perform while in a trance state. A musical ensemble called a *gamelan* encourages the audience to dance along with them. Traditionally, the assembly would travel around a village, visiting people's homes to drive away malevolent spirits. The Barong Dance used to take place once a year in a ten-day festival. Today in Gianyar, it is held publicly for tourists on an almost daily basis.

CALON ARANG

In Balinese mythology, Calon Arang is a terrifying ogress who embodies chaos and destruction. She is portrayed with long claws and thick, unkempt hair that reaches down to the ground. Her limbs are striped red, white, and black. Her hideous face has bulging red eyes, large tusks, and a long tongue covered in golden flames. She is nicknamed Rangda, which means widow. Calon Arang is the leader of all malevolent supernatural spirits. Her most infamous minions are those called the leaks or leyaks. These monsters disguise themselves in the daytime as humans or animals such as pigs. At night the leyaks fly through the air as disembodied heads with their entrails dangling. They feed on corpses, attack pregnant women, and cause disease. Their grotesque faces resemble Calon Arang's.

According to a popular legend, Calon Arang was once human long ago. She was a witch and the widowed mother of a daughter. Yet, her dark sorcery was so infamous that no man wanted to marry the daughter. Calon Arang threatened to unleash floods and plagues upon the village if nobody would wed the girl. Eventually one brave man offered his hand in marriage. The wedding was held, but the suitor was actually a spy. He stole Calon Arang's book of spells and turned it over to the king's advisor, a holy man named Empu Bharada. A war then broke out between the evil witch and the holy man. In the ensuing battle, Calon Arang was transformed into her monstrous form, and Empu Bharada became the heroic Barong. This legend is periodically reenacted by Balinese dancers.

DURONG KRAISORN

The ferocious durong kraisorn is a predatory beast from Thai mythology. Named "horse lion" in ancient Bali, this animal has the body of a horse and the head of a lion. Its head appears highly stylized in traditional artwork, bearing little resemblance to an actual lion. The durong kraisorn is depicted with a long muzzle filled with sharp teeth, a fiery crest in place of a mane, and dragon-like underbelly scales on its equine body. It is red in color. Although it is dangerous, the durong kraisorn does not have the opportunity to prey on humans. It can only be found in a mystical forest known as Himmapan. This forest is said to surround the legendary Mount Meru in the Himalayan Mountains, which is located directly beneath the Buddhist Heaven and is inaccessible to mortals.

Many different mythical species are said to flourish in the Himmapan forest. One that is remarkably similar to the durong kraisorn is called the "to thep ussadorn." This predator is also described as having the body of a horse and the head of a lion. Both animals are capable or running very fast and serve a similar ecological role. They are almost the same creature, yet the to thep ussadorn's name indicates that it is based on a different breed of horse than the durong kraisorn. Its head also appears more recognizably feline. Little is written about either one of these species, yet both of them appear in Buddhist temple art in Thailand, alongside many other mythical creatures of Himmapan. All of them are believed to be real inhabitants of the sacred forest far away.

FLYING ELEPHANT

According to Indian folklore, all elephants used to have wings. Imaginably, the tremendous animals would disturb their surroundings every time they descended from flight. Whenever they would settle into a tree, the branches would break loudly, sending debris and pachyderms crashing dramatically to the ground. One day a holy man named Dirghatapas was meditating near an enormous banyan tree. A herd of elephants flew overhead and proceeded to land, one by one, in the branches of the tree. The commotion they produced was so disruptive that Dirghatapas was driven to anger. He cursed the elephants, and all elephants forever, to be grounded for the rest of their days. He declared that the elephant must thenceforth work as a servant of humans.

Flying elephants appear in Thai art, where the creature is called the karin puksa. This species is said to dwell in the legendary forest called Himmapan. Flying elephants also appear on the logos of two Burmese airlines, Yangon Airways and Myanmar Airways International. The latter's version also features horse-like legs and a fish's tail. A golden, winged elephant with bird claws symbolizes the Kutai Kartenegara sultanate, the royalty of the historical Kutai kingdom in Indonesia. In Bali, colorfully painted wooden statues of winged elephants are used to ward away evil spirits. Buddhist myth tells of a legendary breed of domesticated elephant known as the Uposatha. This breed is white in color and is capable of flight. Although it has this ability, it is usually depicted without wings. In all cases, flying elephants are held to be powerful and are seen in a positive light.

GANDABERUNDA

Gandaberunda, or simply Berunda, is a powerful two-headed bird appearing in Indian art. Often depicted symmetrically as a heraldic symbol, this bird resembles the double-headed eagle from European and central Eurasian imperial iconography. It may share an extremely ancient, common ancestral origin with its European counterpart. However, Gandaberunda is not necessarily an eagle. The Indian bird is depicted with feather crests on its heads, like those of a peacock. It may also have elongated tail feathers, colorful plumage, and other stylized characteristics. Gandaberunda is known for its immense strength and power. It is often portrayed clutching elephants, lions, or other powerful beasts in its claws. This bird was the official emblem of the Wodeyar kingdom of Mysore, which lasted from 1578 to 1947. It also appears on the modern emblem of Karnataka, flanked by a pair of yalis.

A famous myth featuring Gandaberunda concerns a battle between the gods Vishnu and Shiva. Normally allies, the two gods took turns transforming into beasts and, in the process, lost control of their true selves. The story began when Vishnu incarnated into a lion-headed form named Narasimha in order to fight a villain named Hiranyakashipu. Narasimha is often worshipped as a god himself, yet according to the myth, he went mad with bloodlust and posed a threat to the universe. Shiva stepped in to stop Narasimha, which he achieved by transforming into a mythical creature called the Sharabha. But according to some versions of the story, the Sharabha himself also went out of control. Narasimha then turned into Gandaberunda, in which form he was able to defeat the Sharabha, thus saving Shiva and the world.

GARUDA

The bird-like demigod named Garuda is perhaps the most famous mythical creature from India. He is humanoid in shape, with the beak, wings, tail, and claws of a kite or eagle. According to the great Indian epic, the *Mahabharata*, Garuda was so large and burning with fiery energy when he first hatched from his egg that all the gods were terrified. The gods begged him for mercy until he shrank down to a more reasonable size.

In Garuda's first act of heroism, he freed his mother from enslavement by her sister, Kadru, and the 1,000 serpents that served her. Lord Vishnu was so impressed by Garuda's bravery that he granted him immortality. In exchange, Garuda was to serve Vishnu as his *vahana*, or mount, for the rest of eternity. Garuda also became the eternal enemy of serpents and nagas. He had six sons who were all eagles that preyed on serpents.

In Hinduism, Garuda is known as the lord of all birds. In Buddhism, he and his sons begat an entire race of bird-like humanoid beings. These are known as the Suparnas, or simply the Garudas. These supernatural beings dwell in a mystical realm where they have their own cities and four kings. Each Garuda has a wingspan of hundreds of miles, although they are able to shrink down in size. They may take the shape of ordinary eagles or humans. They are warriors who battle against evil beings such as the asuras. Garuda is also an important symbol in various other countries in South Asia. The national emblems of Thailand and Indonesia bear his image.

JATAYU

Jatayu is an enormous, intelligent bird capable of speech. In Indian art he is portrayed as a giant vulture, yet in Southeast Asia he is always depicted with prominent sharp teeth and colorful plumage. Sometimes he is given human-like features. Jatayu and his older brother, Sampati, were the sons of Aruna, the charioteer of the sun god. The two birds once had a flying contest when they were young. Jatayu flew up so high that he was in danger of being burned up by the sun. Sampati quickly flew up to protect him, which resulted in the sun burning off his wings. Sampati fell to the ground and never saw his brother again.

Jatayu later became the king of all birds. He lived for thousands of years. During his lifetime he rescued a man falling from the sky. The man turned out to be a king named Dasaratha. This king went on to have a son named Rama, who was actually the earthly incarnation of Lord Vishnu.

Eventually, Rama's wife, Sita, would be abducted by Ravana, the Rakshasa overlord. Jatayu witnessed the abduction and swiftly pursued Ravana's chariot. He attacked the wicked tyrant and fought him relentlessly. However, Ravana could not be killed by any animal, due to a heavenly boon that made him almost immortal. The villain raised his sword and sliced off Jatayu's wings. Soon, Prince Rama discovered Jatayu on the ground, mortally wounded. Jatayu told Rama what direction Ravana had taken Sita, and then he died. Rama ensured that Jatayu would attain *moksha*, or liberation. This rare honor is the Hindu equivalent of going to Heaven.

KAMADHENU

Kamadhenu is the divine mother of all cows in Indian mythology. In artwork she frequently appears as a white cow with a woman's head and colorful wings. She is usually depicted with a peacock's tail in addition to a regular cow's tail, and human breasts in addition to an udder. Her composite form is the product of Persian influence, reminiscent of the Persian image of the angelic horse al-Buraq.

In other renderings, Kamadhenu is shaped like a regular cow, yet enormous in size. Her body represents Heaven and contains all the different Hindu deities. Her eyes represent the sun and moon, and her legs are the Himalayan Mountains. Others say her legs symbolize the four Vedas, and her teats symbolize four holy texts called the Purusharthas. The name "Kamadhenu" is an epithet meaning "from whom all that is desired is drawn." She has multiple other names and is also known as the Cow of Plenty. In Hindu myth she is known to grant wishes.

The *Mahabharata* states that Kamadhenu originated when the gods churned the cosmic Ocean of Milk to obtain the elixir of life. However, according to the *Devi Bhagavat Purana*, it was she who produced the Ocean of Milk. Kamadhenu's milk is a magical nectar that creates and sustains life. As the mother of all cattle, she cries when she sees bovine animals being mistreated. Hindu religion holds cows to be sacred and forbids people from killing them. Cows are regarded as infinitely benevolent, as they selflessly provide milk, labor, and fertilizer to humans. Some Hindus think of every cow as a manifestation of Kamadhenu.

KINNARA

According to Hindu and Buddhist folklore, the kinnaras are an exotic race that dwells deep in the forests of the Himalayas. In India they are said to be part horse, yet throughout Southeast Asia they are imagined as part bird. They have a human torso and the wings and lower bodies of a goose or swan. Frequently seen in temple art of Southeast Asia, the kinnaras are peaceful musicians, singers, and dancers. Archetypes of romance, they are usually depicted in male-female pairs. The female is called a kinnari.

A famous Southeast Asian fairy tale stars a kinnari princess named Manora, or Manohara. This tale has been adapted into a popular ballet in Thailand. Manora was princess of a golden city called Suwan Nakan. One day she took off her wings and tail to bathe and was then abducted by a hunter. He gave her as a bride to a human prince in a kingdom far away. The prince was named Sutone, and eventually Manora fell in love with him.

One day Sutone went away to war. A corrupted law minister told the royal family that they must sacrifice Manora in a fire in order to ensure Sutone's safety. Manora was allowed one last dance in her traditional clothing. She then rediscovered her wings and tail and flew back home to Suwan Nakan. Eventually the war was over, and Sutone went out to the forest to look for her. When he found her they got remarried in the kinnaras' kingdom. Manora went back to live with Sutone again, but she was allowed to keep her wings and tail on and visit her family whenever she wished.

MACCHANU

Macchanu, or Matchanu, is a unique being in the *Ramakien*, the Thai version of the *Ramayana*. Macchanu has the upper body of an anthropomorphic monkey and the tail of a fish. His father was the monkey demigod Hanuman, and his mother was a mermaid-like being named Supanna Maccha. Macchanu does not appear in most Indian versions of the *Ramayana*, as Hanuman is celibate in Indian literature. But in one version of the story, Hanuman inadvertently produces a son after a drop of his sweat falls into the water. Macchanu's Indian counterpart is named Makardhwaja.

In the Thai *Ramakien*, Hanuman had a brief love affair with the mermaid, Supanna Maccha, daughter of the rakshasa king, Totsakan. When Supanna Maccha gave birth to Macchanu, she abandoned him on the beach to hide him from her father. There he was adopted by another powerful rakshasa named Maiyarab. Maiyarab, King of the Underworld, assigned Macchanu to be the guardian of a pond. Macchanu eventually met his true father on the bank of this pond.

Hanuman was out on a quest to destroy Maiyarab. Suddenly he was stopped by the strange fish-monkey, who ordered him not to proceed. The two of them then engaged in battle, Macchanu proving to be just as strong as Hanuman. Soon they stopped fighting and realized their relation to each other. Hanuman then asked Macchanu how he could reach Maiyarab's castle. Macchanu wanted to help his father, yet he was not allowed to betray Maiyarab. Instead he gave him the answer indirectly, in the form of a riddle. With this clue, Hanuman was able to locate and slay the underworld ruler.

MAHISHASURA

Known as the Buffalo Demon, Mahishasura was an infamous villain from Hindu mythology. *Mahisha* means buffalo in Sanskrit. His mother was a water buffalo, and his father belonged to an antagonistic class of demigods called the asuras. Generally, asuras are thought to look human-like, yet they have the ability to shapeshift. Mahishasura could take the form of numerous animals, the water buffalo being his favorite. He is often depicted as a man with buffalo horns or a buffalo's head. Occasionally he is portrayed with four legs and a human torso, like a centaur.

Mahishasura performed a penance to Agni, the god of fire, and was granted a handsome reward. Per his request he became invincible against any animal or man, mortal or divine. He then waged war against the gods and proceeded to take over the universe. The gods were unable to stop Mahishasura.

Finally, the three major gods, Brahma, Vishnu, and Shiva, joined forces. They produced a brilliant light that took the shape of a woman: Durga, the warrior goddess. Durga went out into battle riding on the back of a tiger, wielding the weapons of all the gods. Mahishasura saw her and demanded that she submit to him as his bride. Durga merely laughed at him, causing an earthquake. She then slaughtered his entire army. Mahishasura fought by transforming into various animals, but she eventually killed him. However, many residents of Mirzapur, India, believe that a reincarnated version of Mahishasura lives in Lake Barewa. Called Bhainsasura, this giant buffalo-headed monster must be appeased with the sacrifice of a pig each year or else he will destroy their crops.

MAKARA

The makara is a fantastical aquatic creature that appears in Indian and other South Asian architectural artwork. Its symbolic presence has been known to Hindu and Buddhist peoples since at least 350 BCE. The makara resembles a composite of various animals. In the earliest known representations, it looked somewhat like a crocodile with an elongated, upward-curled snout. Over time this snout became more exaggerated, coming to resemble an elephant's trunk curled above the animal's head. It has a gaping mouth with long sharp teeth, as well as a fish-like tail that is also curled upward. In later depictions, the tail became peacock feathers or a stylized bush. Makaras can have either two or four short legs. They may also have characteristics of other animals, such as ram's horns.

Although it looks fearsome, the makara is associated with sexuality and fertility, and therefore also with love. Silver bracelets carved to look like makaras are a traditional bridal gift in Hindu weddings. These animals are also believed to possess *rasa*, or juice, which can increase male virility and make men more alluring to women. A makara's mouth contains a magical pearl, which if possessed by a man will enable him to woo the woman of his dreams. This creature appears as the temple crest of Kamadeva, the Hindu god of love. Additionally, Lord Vishnu wears earrings shaped like makaras. Varuna, the god of water, and Ganga, the goddess of the Ganges River, both ride on a makara's back. Water spouts on Tibetan Buddhist temple rooftops are sometimes shaped like makaras. South Asians also interpret the zodiac sign Capricorn as this species.

MATSYA

The word *matsya* simply means fish in Sanskrit. In Hindu religion, the proper name refers to a temporary form assumed by the mighty god Vishnu. Vishnu is said to have had ten earthly incarnations, or avatars, and Matsya was the first of these. Sometimes this avatar is represented by Vishnu emerging from the jaws of a giant fish, causing him to resemble a merman. Yet in other depictions, Matsya appears as a tremendous fish with a horn on its head.

There are many versions of the story of Matsya, the earliest known example appearing in a 3,000-year-old text called the *Satapatha Brahmana*. This tale is a flood myth and may have a common origin with the Hebrew story of Noah. The Indian flood myth began when a tiny Matsya jumped into the hands of a man called Manu. The fish spoke to him and warned him of the coming of a deadly flood. If Manu were to keep and care for the fish and do what it said, he would remain safe.

Manu raised the fish until it grew very large. Following its instruction, he built a great wooden boat. In the oldest version, Manu tethered the boat to a tree. In later versions, Matsya has a horn, and the boat was tethered to his horn. When the floodwaters rose, Manu meditated on the fish while taking refuge on the boat. The enormous Matsya protected the boat over the course of the flood. Matsya also taught great spiritual wisdom to Manu during this time, which is detailed in a Hindu holy text called the *Matsya Purana*.

MERLION

The majestic Singa-Laut, or Merlion, was designed in 1964 to symbolize the island nation of Singapore. Having a lion's head and a fish's body, it combines the two animals that have been historically associated with the progressive city-state. Singapore means "Lion City" (*singa-pura*) in Sanskrit. Singapore was also traditionally a fishing city. There are now seven monumental Merlion statues throughout the city-state. The largest of these was erected in 1995 on the islet of Sentosa. This eleven-story colossus overlooks the city from a pedestal rising nearly 200 feet above sea level. Visitors can go inside and view the city's magnificent skyline from the Merlion's perspective. This statue is lined with thousands of lights and projects multicolored laser beams from its eyes after dark.

Known as the Guardian of Prosperity, the enormous Merlion of Sentosa Island has inspired a new myth. According to this legend, the creature has protected Singapore since ancient times, when the city used to be called Temasek. Every year, the Merlion would visit the island to drive away any threatening forces. One day, a dark and brutal storm ravaged the world and loomed above Temasek as its next target. The great Merlion used its magical powers against the thunder and lightning until the skies were clear and the city was safe. After this, the Merlion was invited to remain on the island forever. It took up its new throne on Sentosa, where it surveys the skies to keep Singapore safe. The storm in this myth may be a metaphor for the Asian financial crisis of 1997. Singapore has remained economically strong, thanks in part to tourism drawn in by the Merlion.

NAGA

The shapeshifting snake-like beings called nagas are one of the most famous of South Asian mythical creatures. This race inhabits kingdoms of paradise unseen by mortals, such as the underworld Patala or the legendary Mount Meru. They are nature spirits associated with water, rain, fertility, and sexuality. Two of their common forms are the multi-headed giant cobra and the half-human, half-snake. They may also assume the shape of ordinary snakes or full human beings. When humanoid, they wear a crown of seven hooded cobra heads or are depicted with seven cobra heads rising up from behind them, reflecting their true nature. In Southeast Asia, nagas are almost always depicted as serpentine, and their faces are highly stylized. A horn-like projection marks each of their heads like a crown. Naga characters in myth are usually either kings or princesses.

Nagas are complex magical beings capable of both good and evil. Book 1 of the *Mahabharata* portrays them negatively as the children of the wicked Kadru. Yet, one of Kadru's children, Sesha, renounced the deeds of his siblings and became a cosmic protector. Sesha grew into a gigantic serpent with a hundred heads and now supports all the planets, including Earth. Another benevolent naga was Mucalinda, who sheltered Buddha from the rain. He spread out his seven hoods like an umbrella and protected Buddha as he meditated under the bodhi tree. The naga princess, Naga Kanya, is a protector of hidden treasure and esoteric teachings in Tibetan Buddhism. She appears in half-human form, with wings, a serpent's tail, and a five-hooded crown. Some Indians refer to regular cobras as nagas and worship them in temples.

NAVAGUNJARA

As with several other fantastic creatures in Hindu mythology, Navagunjara is the shapeshifted form of a god. The god in question is Krishna, who in turn is an avatar or incarnation of Lord Vishnu. This amazing creature appears in a version of the *Mahabharata* that comes from the Indian state of Odisha. Navagunjara is a chimerical being composed of nine different species. It has the head of a rooster, the neck of a peacock, one front limb of a human being, one front limb of an elephant, one hind limb of a tiger, one hind limb of a deer, the back hump of a bull, the midsection of a lion, and a cobra for a tail. This creature is depicted at the Jagannath Temple in Puri, Odisha.

The mythical hero Arjuna encountered Navagunjara while on a hunting trip. Terrified at first, Arjuna prepared to shoot the creature with an arrow. Suddenly he noticed that it had a human arm holding a lotus flower, and he lowered his weapon. He realized that the fantastic beast must be a manifestation of the divine. Navagunjara is generally regarded as part of Krishna's Vishvarupa, or omnipotent form. In this form, the god teaches Arjuna that the ultimate reality is singular, yet it appears differently to different people. The human mind is finite and the universe exceeds that which the mind is capable of perceiving. The name Navagunjara can be translated as "nine venerable qualities." The nine different animals in its composition may hold specific allegorical meanings, yet if so, these meanings are not commonly known.

RAKSHASA

The rakshasas are a prominent race of monstrous humanoids from Hindu mythology. They also appear in Buddhist myth and folklore outside India. They may have originated as a caricature of foreign enemy peoples faced by ancient Vedic storytellers. Rakshasas are depicted with grotesque features such as fiery red eyes, fangs, claws, and, occasionally, animal heads. They also have supernatural powers, including shapeshifting, flight, and the ability to change their size. Embodying greed, these beings are often regarded as predators of human flesh. A small minority of them are benevolent. Frequently labeled as demons in English, this race is sometimes confused with other subversive beings, particularly the asuras. The asuras dwell in the celestial realm while the rakshasas are confined to Earth. Some sources suggest that a rakshasa is a type of asura.

The king of the rakshasas in the classical Hindu epic, the *Ramayana*, was named Ravana. He had ten heads and twenty arms, although he could also assume a normal human shape. Long ago, Ravana had performed a penance to the god Shiva and received great power in return. As a result, he became invulnerable against any god, spirit, or animal. Only a human could kill him, yet he believed humans to be too weak to pose any threat. He then proclaimed himself the most powerful being in the universe. Later, Ravana made the mistake of abducting Sita, the wife of Prince Rama. Unbeknown to him, Rama was actually the earthly incarnation of the god Vishnu. Since he was human, Rama was eventually able to slay Ravana. Thus, the gods outwitted Ravana and restored the universe to its natural order.

SHARABHA

The Sharabha is one of the most unusual creatures in Hindu mythology. Its name could refer to a number of animals in ancient Sanskrit, including a mythical beast with eight limbs. This creature's appearance is not widely agreed upon, yet it is unequivocally powerful and fierce. Four of its limbs point downward and four point upward, possibly suggesting a centaur-shaped beast with four arms. It is sometimes also said to have four eyes. The Buddhist version of the Sharabha is regarded as a type of deer, in keeping with one of the older Sanskrit uses of its name. Yet, Hindu depictions of the mythical creature are usually composite in nature, often with a lion-like form at its base. Ancient Vedic texts portray the Sharabha as an alpha predator of the forest. It is able to kill lions, leap over elephants, and terrify all animals with its roar.

The Sharabha is best known as an avatar of the god Shiva. An extremely complex god, Shiva embodies destructive forces as well as creative and benevolent powers. According to Shaivist scripture, Shiva once transformed into the Sharabha in a battle against Narasimha. Narasimha was a lion-headed avatar of Vishnu who had gone mad with bloodlust. Most of the texts state that Shiva assumed a bird-like version of Sharabha, equipped with wings and a beak. He is referred to as Sharabeshamurti when in this form. Upon seeing this being, Narasimha fainted or became paralyzed with fear. Sharabha then separated Vishnu from his monstrous form, flayed and decapitated Narasimha, and discarded his body on a distant mountain. Vishnu was then able to return to his normal righteous self.

SINGA

The singa, or singha, is a fabled symbol of strength and protection in Indonesia and Thailand. The word *singa* actually means "lion" in Sanskrit. But wild lions do not exist in Southeast Asia, and the lion was therefore perceived in a mythical context. Ancient peoples did not even necessarily know what lions looked like. In traditional Thai artwork, these animals have stylized heads that look little like actual lions. Some variants may possess unusual features such as hooves. They are all believed to reside in the legendary Himmapan forest alongside other mythical creatures. According to some sources, the king of the beasts in Himmapan is a singha called Rajasi or Rajasri, whose mane is made of fire.

Indonesia is home to some even more fantastical singas. In the province of Bali, the singa is a highly ornate creature with wings and horns. It also has elongated fangs or tusks, and the round, bulging eyes commonly attributed to supernatural beings. Its tail is covered in stylized spikes, which may represent hair or fire. Its image is usually seen in apotropaic contexts, meaning that it is believed to drive away evil spirits.

Among the Batak tribes of North Sumatra, the name *singa* is applied to a completely different-looking mythical creature that also serves an apotropaic purpose. Highly stylized, it sports a human-like face and a long, scaly body. It has the horns of a buffalo, the tail of a fish, and two to four legs with hooves, yet usually only the head is portrayed. Despite its name, this creature is thought to actually be based on a naga from Hindu mythology.

TOYOL

Malaysian folklore describes a small humanoid monster called a toyol or tuyul. Generally, this creature is said to be the same size and shape as a human infant, yet with ghoulish features. In recent times it has become popularly depicted as green-skinned and pointy-eared, with large red eyes. This image may have been influenced by Western goblins and aliens from movies. Some descriptions also give it sharp teeth, claws, hairy skin, and other grotesque characteristics. Toyols are commonly thought to be the transfigured forms of aborted and miscarried fetuses, or children who died before baptism. These undead creatures are not very intelligent and live in the forest like animals. With the exception of certain regional variants, they pose little threat to humans when left to their own devices.

Witch doctors called *bomohs* are infamous for calling in toyols to use as minions. Clients can pay a bomoh for the services of a toyol. The creature's master must appease it with toys, sweets, cups of milk, or even blood. In return, it can be sent to bring disease and misfortune upon others. Toyols can also enable their masters to become rich. They accomplish this primarily by stealing money and possessions from other people. Individuals who have an unfair advantage over others, especially wealthy business magnates, are often rumored to have toyols at their service. Toyols are also blamed for unexplainable mishaps, much like European goblins and pixies. Occasionally they are said to steal babies and turn them into toyols. Folklore of these and similar diminutive monsters exists throughout many Southeast Asian countries.

YALI

The yali is a fearsome yet righteous beast seen in southern Indian and Sri Lankan art. Its name is derived from the Sanskrit *vyala*, meaning "fierce creature." It is a composite or chimerical animal with the body of a lion, combined with attributes of other animals. Most of them have horns. Many yalis have an elephant trunk. Others may have a long, curly tongue, or a lotus plant extending from their mouth in place of a trunk. Oftentimes the yali's head is uniquely grotesque and cannot be identified with any real animal. Some may also have hooves, a serpent's tail, or other chimerical features. Despite the variability in their appearance, all yalis are considered sacred and are recognized for their function as temple guardians. One legend states that the yali once posed a threat to the world but was subdued and converted by Lord Vishnu.

Yalis are best known from carvings on temple architecture, especially in the states of Tamil Nadu and Karnataka. The beasts are usually seen carved into pillars and depicted rearing up on their hind legs. They often stand atop an elephant, which is small compared to the yali. The yali's ability to dwarf an elephant reflects its awesome strength and symbolizes divine power. The creature is shown protecting the elephant rather than harming it. Yali Cave in Mahabalipuram, Tamil Nadu, features eleven feline yali heads with horns and tusks, arranged in a semicircle around the temple's entrance. Two elephant-headed yalis also appear on the government emblem of the state of Karnataka. These beasts are sometimes identified with the Sharabha and the god Shiva.

YETI

One of the most famous cryptids in the world, the proper yeti comes from the folklore of the Himalayan Sherpas in Nepal. The cryptid's name means "that thing" or "that creature." It had formerly been mistranslated as "abominable snowman"; hence its alternative name in English. Contrary to popular misconception, the ape-like beast is not traditionally said to be white in color. The Sherpas recognize three different kinds of yetis. One of these is the *meh-teh*, meaning "human-like thing." This type is human-sized, about 5–6 feet tall. Its fur is reddish brown to black and may have white markings. The second kind is called the *dzu-teh*, meaning "big thing." Significantly larger than a human, this massive beast has long fangs and is sometimes said to walk on all fours. The third kind is called *teh-lma*, meaning "little thing." It is about 3–4 feet tall, covered with thick reddish fur, and has a conical head.

The yeti became a popular cryptid in the West after Western explorers began reporting sightings of these creatures and their footprints. Sherpas consider the yeti to be a sacred mystical being, yet Americans and Brits saw it as an unknown species awaiting scientific discovery. Eagerly hunting for evidence, Westerners broke apart and stole a piece of a sacred mummified yeti hand from a Buddhist temple in Pangboche, Nepal. Following the results of a DNA test in 2011, scientists concluded that the hand was human. Other purported tissue and hair samples have been identified as coming from bears and a goat-like animal called a serow. Footprints photographed in 1951 are thought to be different overlapping animal tracks that were distorted by melting snow.

Chapter Nine

EAST ASIA

H ome to some of the world's earliest civilizations, East Asia is a major seat of historic achievement and global influence. The region is dominated by China, the world's largest country in terms of population, and the world's oldest continuous civilization. This extraordinary nation produced some of antiquity's greatest rulers, engineers, scientists, warriors, artists, shipbuilders, and philosophers. It is the birthplace of rice, silk, domesticated pigs, paper, printing, explosives, and many other important inventions. Chinese culture has strongly influenced neighboring countries: Japan, Korea, Tibet, Taiwan, and Vietnam. This chapter focuses primarily on the mythology of China and Japan.

East Asia may be richer in mythical creatures than any other region of the world. China alone boasts hundreds of creatures from ancient bestiaries. The most famous bestiary is the *Shan Hai Jing*, or the *Classic of Mountains and Seas*, compiled over 2,000 years ago. It describes some 500 imaginative species, as well as hundreds of legendary mountains, rivers, plants, and medicines. Numerous Chinese mythical animals have been adopted by other East Asian countries. Japan is even more famous for its imaginary creatures. Japanese monsters and other strange beings are known collectively as yokai. Unlike the creatures it borrowed from China, the yokai are uniquely Japanese. Japan has also developed newer monsters; these include kaiju from movies such as *Godzilla* as well as the more recent *Pokémon*™.

AMIKIRI

The amikiri is one of the strangest-looking of all yokai, or Japanese monsters. This creature vaguely resembles a shrimp. Its body is elongated, almost serpentine, and is segmented with an exoskeleton. It has two long arms equipped with sharp, pincer-like claws. Its mouth is a beak and its eyes resemble those of a bird or mammal, rather than a shrimp's compound eyes. It is also usually depicted as having hair on its head. The amikiri is larger than a normal shrimp, yet relatively small for a monster. It is thought to have originated from the ocean, although it is not confined to the water. Traditional Japanese artwork depicts this creature traveling by floating through the air.

The name *amikiri* means "net cutter." The word *ami* means both "net" and a type of shrimp, thus indicating a pun as the probable basis of the myth. As its name implies, the amikiri is notorious for cutting fishing nets with its claws, thus releasing the fisherman's catch. It is unclear whether this yokai wants to eat the sea creatures or set them free, but either way it is a nuisance to humans. Folklore has further elaborated upon the amikiri's antics by also having it float into people's houses through open windows. It not only cuts fishing nets but also mosquito nets, and occasionally clotheslines as well. It is related to another yokai called the kamikiri, or "hair cutter." This species also sports sharp pincers and a beak yet has a more humanoid body. Both of these beings enter people's homes in search of things to cut, yet neither one inflicts direct physical injury upon humans.

BAI ZE

The bai ze of Chinese mythology is a white-furred beast with a human-like head. Its body is usually described as bovine, although earlier versions were more lion-like. It has nine eyes: three on its face and three on either side of its body. It also has up to three horns growing from each of its sides. The bai ze is a holy creature rumored to dwell on a mountain called Dongwang. Huangdi, the legendary Yellow Emperor, is said to have had a conversation with this being sometime around 2600 BCE. The bai ze iterated the names of 11,520 monsters, spirits, and supernatural beings, along with information on how to protect oneself from them. All this information was recorded in a book known as the *Bai Ze Tu*, which has since been lost.

The bai ze was imported into Japan, where it is known as the hakutaku. It became a popular protective symbol during the Edo period, its image being believed to repel evil yokai and malicious forces. The hakutaku is often confused with a more recently conceived mythical creature called the kudan. The latter has a bovine body and a human face, yet no extra eyes or horns. Japanese folklore tells of a human-faced bovine that appeared on the holy mountain Tateyama in the Toyama Prefecture. The strange beast prophesized that a terrible plague would soon befall the land. It instructed the people to use its image as a talisman that could ward away sickness. This creature was called the kutabe and has been identified with both the hakutaku and the kudan in different sources.

BAKU

The baku has a Japanese name but is believed to have originated in China first. As with many Chinese mythical creatures, yet unlike most Japanese ones, this species is considered benevolent, auspicious, and holy. Its appearance is a combination of several animals. It possesses an elephant trunk and tusks, the eyes of a rhino, the mane of a lion, the legs of a tiger, the body of a bear, and the tail of an ox. Sometimes it is depicted with spotted fur. According to legend, the gods created the baku after they finished creating all the other animals. They assembled the creature by using all the pieces they had left over. Today, the Japanese identify the baku with a real-life animal called the Malayan tapir (*Tapirus indicus*).

The baku is a protector of humankind and devourer of evil spirits. The Japanese believe that malevolent spirits can cause people to have nightmares. A nightmare is not merely a fantasy, but a supernatural attack that can cause a person to have bad luck throughout the day. The baku is best known as the destroyer of the spirits that produce nightmares. When it eats these spirits it is said to be eating the nightmares themselves. It is sometimes known by the epithet *yumekui*, or "dream eater." The image of the baku is apotropaic, meaning it can be used to ward off evil. People in Japan used to embroider the kanji, representing its name onto pillows to prevent nightmares. If a person has a bad dream, they may call upon the baku as soon as they wake up, thus banishing any evil that may be lingering about them.

CHAN CHU
(MONEY FROG)

The chan chu from Chinese mythology is better known in English as the money frog or money toad. It is also known as jin chan, meaning golden toad. The creature may be either a frog or a toad, as the Chinese language does not draw a distinction. Its appearance suggests a toad, as it has bumpy skin, which is encrusted with jewels. The chan chu is also distinct for having only three legs; one of its hind legs is absent. This amphibian often appears in the form of a figurine or statue placed inside a home or business. It sits atop a pile of Chinese coins and holds one large coin in its mouth. These statues are used in feng shui to attract wealth.

The chan chu is associated with the moon. According to one legend, it is the transfigured form of the moon goddess named Chang-O or Chang'e. She became a goddess after stealing and consuming a pill of immortality that was intended for her husband, Houyi. Chang'e fled to the moon, where she now resides. Houyi, also called Shenyi or simply Yi, was later granted immortality in the sun as the three-legged crow. These two three-legged creatures represent *yin* and *yang*. In a similar account, the wife of one of the Eight Immortals stole the Peaches of Immortality and was turned into the three-legged toad as a punishment. The chan chu is also an attribute of the legendary alchemist named Liu Hai or Liu Haichan. This figure is said to have learned the secret of immortality from the toad and is now considered a god of wealth.

DRAGON, ASIAN

Despite its name in English, the Asian "dragon" is completely unrelated to the true dragon of Western mythology. The most powerful creature in Asian myth is properly called Long in Chinese, Yong in Korean, Rông in Vietnamese, and Tatsu or Ryu in Japanese. It is a celestial being, originating in ancient China as a god of rain, wind, and thunder. Able to control the flow of water, it was responsible for the fertility of the land, the bounty of crops, and the prosperity of the harvest. It has the magical ability to fly, yet its standard form is wingless. The Asian dragon is frequently depicted guarding a fiery pearl or orb. Symbolizing omnipotent power, this orb may represent the Cintamani in Buddhist tradition. Chinese mythology portrays the dragon as a benevolent being, although Japanese mythology sometimes differs.

It has been suggested that the Asian dragon originated as a composite of the totem animals of different Chinese tribes that were unified under the Yellow Emperor. In general, this being is a symbol of the Chinese emperor and is associated with Chinese ethnic identity. The Imperial Dragon specifically has five toes on each foot; lesser variants have four or even three. It can appear in various colors, with the Imperial form usually being either gold or blue. A blue or azure dragon has particular celestial significance and is identified as the most powerful of the heavenly guardians. The Asian dragon also appears in the Chinese zodiac. Persons born in the year of the dragon are said to be confident, ambitious, energetic, and naturally suited for leadership.

FENGHUANG

An extremely ancient motif, the fenghuang is one of the most magical creatures in Chinese mythology. It is a wondrous bird often labeled in English as the Chinese phoenix. In actuality, the fenghuang is not a phoenix. The Chinese celestial bird is immortal but does not undergo a cycle of death and rebirth. It is a symbol of virtue and an omen of peace and good tidings. It is shaped like an elongated chicken or pheasant with long tail plumes like a peacock. The male, called the *feng*, has five tail plumes, while the female, called the *huang*, has two. Its feathers bear the five sacred colors: red, yellow, blue, black, and white. These colors correspond to the five virtues of Confucianism. Its head represents virtue or knowledge; its wings, duty; its back, propriety; its breast, benevolence; and its belly, integrity.

The male feng is associated with the sun, and the female huang with the lunar cycle. The male and female are typically depicted alongside one another as a representation of *yin* and *yang*. Additionally, the fenghuang frequently appears with the Asian dragon, signifying *yin* contrasted with the dragon's *yang*. This pairing is sometimes used at weddings to symbolize a happy marriage. The fenghuang is one of the Four Benevolent Animals, the other three being the dragon, the qilin, and the tortoise. This species is known in Korea as the bonghwang, in Vietnam as the phụng, and in Japan as the ho-o. It replaces the rooster in the zodiac in Korea and certain parts of China. Sometimes it is confused with the zhu que or vermillion bird, which is a constellation.

FU DOGS

A type of guardian lion, the Fu dogs possess attributes of both lion and dog. Lions provide the basis of several mythical creatures in Asia, especially of the protective variety. Wild lions never existed in East Asia and were therefore historically perceived as mystical beings. Fu dogs always appear in pairs, usually as statues guarding the entrance of a building or compound. They are associated with Buddhism and are also called Buddha dogs or lion dogs. In Japan they are known as shishi and komainu, while in Tibet they are called snow lions. The shiisa of Okinawa is regarded as the same creature, yet it may have arrived in the region separately, via influence from Southeast Asia.

Male and female Fu dogs appear side by side, representing *yin* and *yang*. Their role is to prevent evil spirits from entering a building. The male always has his mouth open, ready to swallow the evil spirits, while the female's mouth is closed to prevent the spirits from escaping. The male is also portrayed holding a globe beneath his paw, while the female guards a tiny cub. Both sexes have a mane.

Folklore holds that Buddha was able to tame the savage lion and was thenceforth guarded by a pair of them as though they were dogs. Due to this legend, and the fact that most people in ancient China did not know what lions looked like, lions became conflated with dogs. Dog breeders produced the Pekingese and Lhasa Apso to resemble these sacred creatures. Pekingese dogs were once considered embodiments of Buddha's lions. For centuries, only royalty and courtiers were allowed to own them.

HAETAE

The haetae, also spelled haitai, is a variant of guardian lion popular in South Korea. Originally this creature came from Chinese folklore, where it is known as xiezhi. It blends characteristics of the Fu dogs and the qilin. Typically described as a lion with a horn, the haetae appears in a number of different forms. The Chinese version may closely resemble the qilin, sometimes bearing hooves. Its body is often covered with scales. Yet, like the Fu dogs, it is also considered dog-like, especially in Korean art. Sometimes the creature's horn is reduced to a mere button. It is also depicted with a bell at its throat.

The haetae is known for two things: its unwavering sense of justice and its ability to thwart natural disasters. As per ancient Chinese myth, this beast is said to identify wrongdoers and butt them with its horn. It can also extinguish fires by eating the flames. The haetae was used as a symbol of justice and protection during the Joseon dynasty of Korea, from 1392 to 1897. Statues of the creature were erected outside the palace of Gyeongbokgoong to protect it from damage from forest fires. Their presence also reminded government officials to rule morally and justly.

In 2008, the government of Seoul, South Korea, decided that the haetae would become the city's new official mascot. As such, it is more popularly known by its alternative name, Haechi. This mascot was chosen because of its historical significance and its potential for versatility in marketing. Modern interpretations of Haechi now appear all over the city in various embellished forms.

JOROGUMO

The golden orb weaver spider (genus *Nephila*) is known as jorogumo in Japanese. According to folklore, this arachnid is a type of *bakemono*, or changing yokai. Once the spider reaches 400 years of age, it grows enormous in size and becomes a deadly shapeshifter. It can then disguise itself as a beautiful woman and seduce human male prey. Sometimes this yokai is portrayed as a horrible monster with the torso of a woman and the lower body of a giant spider. The name *jorogumo* is often translated as "entangling bride," although this is only a euphemism. In the past it was written differently to read "whore spider."

A jorogumo targets men whom she finds attractive. Those looking for love are the most vulnerable. Jorogumos frequently prey on lone travelers out in the woods. There are stories of men falling asleep outdoors and waking up to find spider silk wrapped around their legs. If the man awakens early enough, he may be able to untangle himself and escape.

Other jorogumos live in the city, where they adopt a full-time human identity and live in a house. The jorogumo invites her victims into her home and then ties them up in silk before injecting them with venom. It often takes days for the victim to weaken and die while the sadistic predator relishes in his suffering. A jorogumo's home may contain hundreds of dried and discarded corpses before being discovered. If she thinks she is in danger of being discovered, she may send out her fire-breathing spider minions to burn down the homes of those who suspect her.

KAPPA

One of the most infamous and frequently encountered mythical creatures in Japan, the kappa is a vaguely humanoid reptile or amphibian. It stands at around 3 feet tall and is usually depicted with the shell and beak of a turtle. It also has human-like hair, except for the very top of its head, where its skull caves in like a bowl and is filled with water. Kappas live in the water but are able to survive on land so long as their head cavity remains full. This water endows them with intimidating physical strength and magical powers. Kappas are notorious for their mischievous, malevolent, and sometimes deadly interactions with humans and livestock. Male kappas sometimes assault women. The species feeds on cucumbers and children. They will also eat eggplants, horses, cattle, and human entrails.

There are several ways to thwart a kappa. These creatures can be repelled by iron, deer antlers, monkeys, ginger, and sesame. They may be bribed or distracted with cucumbers. However, the most effective way to subdue this yokai is to cause it to lose the water in its head cavity. Parents tell their children they should bow if they see a kappa. The kappa may feel obligated to return the bow, which will cause its head water to spill. If it loses this water, it will suddenly become very weak and must return to the water quickly, or it may die. Kappas can also be forced into agreements to refrain from tormenting a person's family. A kappa that has entered into such a pact may then share its mystical knowledge. The art of bone-setting was purportedly acquired from a kappa.

KIRIN

—See *Qilin*.

KITSUNE

—See *Nine-Tailed Fox*.

NEKOMATA

The nekomata is a fiendish cat yokai from Japan. It is typically portrayed as an abnormally large house cat that walks on its hind legs and has two tails. Its name has been translated to mean "forked cat," in reference to its tails. However, this creature only became depicted as twin-tailed later in time, and the word *mata* has other meanings besides forked. The original meaning of its name is unclear. During the Kamakura period, from 1185 to 1333, the nekomata was described as a dog-sized mountain cat that preyed on humans. It was regarded as simply a dangerous wild animal rather than a supernatural being. Later, during the Edo period, from 1603 to 1868, the nekomata acquired magical powers and became depicted with two tails.

Today, the nekomata is classified as a type of bakeneko, or changing cat. According to Japanese folklore, all cats have the potential to transform into yokai. Upon transformation, these cats grow larger in size, walk on two legs, and gain the ability to speak. They change naturally after they reach a certain age, although this age varies according to region. A cat that dies after being mistreated will also come back as a nekomata. The nekomata is a sinister and vindictive being, capable of producing magical fire and even reanimating human corpses. It will kill any person who it feels had wronged it. Some nekomata are more bloodthirsty than others, yet all are regarded with fear. People used to cut off cats' tails to prevent them from splitting into two, thus preventing the cat from transforming. There was also caution regarding the length of time that was safe to own a cat.

NIAN

The legend of the Nian in Chinese folklore is also the story of the New Year tradition. The name *Nian* means year. The Chinese New Year festival is called *Guo Nian* in Chinese, which means the "Passing of Nian," symbolized by the defeat of the monster. Chinese communities in the Western world traditionally use a gigantic dragon puppet in their New Year's festivals. However, the version celebrated in China and Vietnam uses the Nian, resembling a stylized giant lion with a horn.

This monster is said to live either at the bottom of the sea or in the mountains, depending on the regional version. The Nian would invade a location called Peach Blossom Village every New Year's Eve, where it would devour humans and livestock. One year a beggar came to Peach Blossom Village while the people were scrambling to hide. He claimed he knew how to scare away the Nian. One old woman gave him food but did not believe him, and she fled for her life.

The man remained at her house when the Nian arrived. When the monster drew near, it was startled to see red paper hanging all over the house. Afraid of the color red, it prepared to attack the house. That was when the old man began beating a gong and lighting firecrackers. The Nian fled in terror, as loud noises were its other fear. When the people returned home they found their village safe, with the old man wearing red and surrounded by burning lamps. The villagers listened to his wisdom then. Now every New Year's Eve is celebrated with firecrackers and the color red.

NINE-TAILED FOX

Nine-tailed foxes exist in the folklore of China, Japan, and other Asian countries. In China they are called jiuweihu. This creature is mentioned in the *Classic of Mountains and Seas*, written during the Han dynasty over 2,000 years ago. This book presents it as a wild animal that dwells in exotic lands populated by other fantastical beings. The *Classic of Mountains and Seas* states that the flesh of the nine-tailed fox, if eaten, can protect people from a deadly insect poison called *gu*. The fox itself is said to prey on humans, yet in Taoism it is considered highly auspicious.

One famous legend mentions a white nine-tailed fox encountered by the heroic emperor Yu the Great. This was interpreted as a sign that he would marry the maiden Niujiao. The nine tails of the fox became recognized as a symbol of having many offspring.

All foxes are traditionally believed to have magical powers, such as shapeshifting into humans, and can potentially take spiritual possession of human victims. Nine-tailed foxes are the most magically adept. Chinese literature indicates that the jiuweihu can be either good or evil. The Korean version of this creature, called the gumiho, is regarded as downright predatory and malevolent. In Japan these beings are infamously mischievous, and their auspicious associations from Chinese Taoism are generally absent. The word *kitsune* refers to all foxes in Japanese, whether they are mundane, nine-tailed, or shapeshifting. Japanese folklore claims that a fox will grow an extra tail if it lives for one hundred years and will gain an additional tail each century until it has nine of them.

NUE

The nue is a composite beast, sometimes called the Japanese chimera by Westerners. It has the head of a Japanese snow monkey, the body of a tanuki or raccoon dog, the legs of a tiger, and a snake for a tail. It also has the voice of a small bird called a White's thrush, which in ancient times was considered an omen of misfortune.

The nue appears in the 1371 epic *Heike Monogatari*, or the *Tale of the Heike*. According to this book, the evil creature used magic to attack Emperor Konoe in the year 1153. The emperor began having nightmares every night. Soon he fell gravely ill. Doctors and priests were unable to cure him. Nights passed and the spiritual onslaught continued.

Then one night at 2:00 a.m., lightning struck the roof of the palace, causing it to catch fire. The desperate emperor summoned his vassal, samurai Yorimasa of the legendary Minamoto clan. Yorimasa waited on the rooftop for the evil spirit to return, accompanied by his sidekick, I no Hayata. Storm clouds gathered once again at 2:00 a.m. Yorimasa shot arrows into the cloud until a wounded nue fell onto the roof. The sidekick Hayata immediately finished off the creature.

By magic, Emperor Konoe instantly recovered from his illness. As a reward, he granted the two heroes a legendary sword called Shishiō. The people placed the slain nue into a boat and floated it down the Kamo River. Later they gave it a respectful burial so as not to incur the wrath of its spirit. Today there are multiple locations said to be its final resting place.

NURE-ONNA

The waters of southern Japan are said to be haunted by the deadly nure-onna. This yokai appears as a massive serpent with a woman's head. Its name means "wet woman." This monster is generally regarded as a sea-dweller, yet some stories place her in freshwater rivers and marshes. Her snake-like body is purportedly hundreds of feet in length. Her human face has protruding fangs and a long, forked tongue. Anyone who looks into her eyes will become paralyzed with fear. Some say she can paralyze with her gaze alone, even if her victim is not looking back at her. Some claim she is one of a kind, while others classify the nure-onna as an entire species.

The nure-onna preys on human males and drinks their blood. She deceives her victims by posing as a perfectly normal, harmless woman. In some versions she has human arms and shoulders and can be seen brushing her hair, with her snake-like body concealed underwater. In other versions she can come out of the water and shapeshift. She is particularly notorious for assuming the form of a young woman holding a baby. She approaches fishermen while in this guise, seemingly very tired, and will ask the man to hold her baby for her. If the man obligingly takes up the baby, it will suddenly transform into a heavy boulder and he will be unable to let go. He thus becomes trapped and the nure-onna claims her next meal. In some accounts, the nure-onna collaborates in her hunting efforts with another seaside predator called the ushi-oni. Sometimes she is said to be married to this monster.

ONI

The oni is a well-known class of Japanese yokai, often identified in English as a demon or ogre. It is an enormous, grotesque humanoid, sporting horns, claws, and long, unkempt hair. Some onis have three eyes or bestial faces. Their skin can be red, blue, or green. They are typically depicted wearing a tiger-skin loincloth and carrying a spiked club called a kanabo. Their Korean counterpart is called a dokkaebi. Earlier versions of the oni were invisible like ghosts and had the ability to shapeshift. These traits are still common among dokkaebi, which behave like mischievous faeries or goblins. The dokkaebi are known to smite humans for their misdeeds and occasionally bring wealth to good people. The Japanese oni became more of a general villain, although some of them serve as guardians.

Onis appear in many myths and fairy tales. Two onis, one red and one green, are said to accompany Enma-O, the ruler of Jigoku, the Japanese Buddhist Hell. These onis' job is to torture and punish the wicked. Onis attack randomly in many folktales, abducting people and even eating them. They also frequently own objects with magical properties. As with European ogres, these beings are extremely strong but not very smart. In most stories, the protagonist escapes from the dim-witted brute by outsmarting it. It is highly unusual for a human to best an oni in combat, yet one popular hero, named Momotaro, managed to do this. The uncanny Momotaro defeated an entire band of onis with the help of his animal friends. Another legendary hero, Minamoto no Yorimitsu, gave poison sake to an oni and then cut off its head.

PIXIU

The pixiu ("pee-shyuh") is a highly auspicious mythical beast from China. It has also been Romanized as bixie and has alternative names of tian lu and pi yao. This creature resembles a lion with small wings and either one or two horns. Sometimes it is hoofed. According to some sources, the male is called the *pi* and has one horn, while the female is called the *xiu* and has two horns. Alternatively, the name tian lu refers specifically to the single-horned form. Some sources include the pixiu among the offspring of the Dragon King, identifying it as the ninth and youngest. Its name has been also used as an epithet given to fierce warriors serving in the army.

The pixiu is known primarily for its abilities to attract wealth and block malevolent energy, as well as its extreme loyalty to its master. Today it is widely used in feng shui, the practice of optimizing energy flow in a house or other space to promote prosperity and balance. Legend holds that the pixiu feeds exclusively and voraciously on gold and silver. It also has no anus, meaning it will never lose the wealth that it draws in. Originally this peculiarity was a punishment for violating a heavenly law, wrought upon the creature by the Jade Emperor. Statues or figurines of the pixiu are believed to attract wealth from all directions. They can also protect their owner from the ill effects of an astrological force known as Tai Sui or Grand Duke. The statue should be respected as a living being because the pixiu's spirit is believed to reside within.

QILIN

The qilin or ch'i-lin is sometimes referred to by Westerners as the Chinese unicorn. In actuality it is unrelated to the unicorn, and the Chinese do not confuse the two. The qilin may have one horn or two. It is a magnificent hoofed animal covered in scales and plumes of fire. Its head is similar to an Asian dragon's. The male is called the *qi* and the female is called the *lin*. It is said to have been the first four-legged mammal.

This creature has spread into the mythology of other Asian countries. Chinese tradition names it as one of the Four Benevolent Animals that dwell in the garden of the Yellow Emperor. The others are the dragon, the fenghuang, and the tortoise. The Japanese call it the kirin and consider it to be the most powerful of all mythical creatures.

This creature is also known to defend the righteous. According to Japanese folklore, it may also stab wrongdoers with its horn.

The qilin is regarded as a prophetic omen of prosperity and serenity. One is said to have appeared before the birth of the great philosopher Confucius. It bore a scroll declaring that the child would possess the wisdom and virtue of the emperor. Women sometimes surround themselves with images of the qilin in hopes that this sacred beast will bring them a child destined for greatness. During the thirteenth century, Chinese emperor Zheng He traveled to East Africa and brought two giraffes back to Beijing. The emperor proclaimed that the animals were qilins, and his possession of them was a sign of his greatness and power.

RAIJU

Raiju is a pet belonging to Raijin, the Shinto (Japanese) god of thunder and lightning. The creature's true appearance is rarely revealed due to its body being wrapped in lightning. It is generally perceived as a carnivorous mammal, often a composite of various species such as wolf, fox, cat, tanuki, and weasel. It is also known to possess characteristically large claws. The sound of thunder may either be its roar or is produced by Raijin beating on a drum. Raiju has no wings but can fly. Lightning manifests in its flight. Its favorite prey is a type of bird called *Kaminari-no-tori*, another supernatural creature associated with lightning. Lightning occurs when Raiju chases these birds through the sky, or when it otherwise becomes agitated. Where lightning has struck, it is said that Raiju has scratched with its claws.

Raiju's home is believed to be on a mountaintop, either on Mount Hakusan or Mount Asama. Strangely, it is also believed to sometimes sleep inside people's belly buttons, especially during storms. Its presence in one's navel is extremely dangerous, as Raijin may throw lightning at the person's abdomen to wake his pet from slumber. Of course, this can be fatal to the person who only happened to be in the wrong place at the wrong time. If one is outdoors during a storm, this hazard can be avoided by lying down in prone position with the belly hidden. People should always avoid trees during lightning storms because Raiju perches in trees. The creature can be repelled with burning incense, mosquito nets, and camels.

SHANGYANG (RAIN BIRD)

The shangyang, or rain bird, is one of many magical birds in Chinese mythology. This bird is characterized by having only one leg. Aside from this, its appearance is not usually described. Most of the time it is the size of a normal bird, yet it has the power to change its size. Sometimes it will become large enough to drink up an entire lake or river, which it then sprays out of its beak in the form of rain. The shangyang is said to accompany the god Yu Shi, the Master of Rain. Other accounts claim it belongs to a rain god named Chisongzi, or Chih Sung-Tzu, who is venerated by peasant farmers. Elsewhere still, it is said to be the familiar of Fei Lian, the god of wind.

According to one tale, the shangyang once appeared in a state known as Qi, or Ch'i. One version of the story states that it flew down and perched on the arm of the prince of Qi. In another version, it simply stood in front of his throne and hopped up and down on its one leg. Realizing that this was some kind of omen, the prince sent for the great sage Confucius to interpret it. Immediately Confucius recognized the gravity of the situation. He warned that they would soon have exceptionally heavy rains. He urged the prince to build a series of channels and dykes in order to prevent catastrophic flooding. The prince heeded the wise man's advice. The downpour struck and Qi was saved, yet the surrounding areas were not so lucky.

TENGU

The tengu are one of the most famous and abundant species of Japanese yokai. They are winged male humanoids known for their martial arts skills and magic powers. Dwelling in the mountains, they dress like monks, especially the Yamabushi monks. There are two races of tengu. The hanadaku ("longnose") tengu, or daitengu, is the more powerful and enlightened class. These appear as winged men with long, bulbous noses and usually have red skin. They resemble Sarutahiko, the Shinto god of martial arts. The lesser race is the karasu ("raven") tengu, or kotengu. These have the heads and claws of birds as well as bodies covered with feathers. They appear earlier in folklore and are more malevolent. Strangely, the name "tengu" comes from the Chinese *tiangou*, referring to a mythical dog.

Tengu are highly complex beings both feared and revered. Their mythology is ancient and extremely rich. Notorious for playing pranks, they may cause their victims to go mad, or pick them up and transport them to distant locations. Karasu-tengu are known to attack people for no apparent reason, while the hanadaku-tengu serve as guardians of monasteries. They generally despise the rich and powerful. In medieval times, tengu were malicious antagonists symbolizing the many obstructions on a soul's path to enlightenment. Over time they became recognized as the reincarnation of monks and priests who were too vain or prideful to go to the Buddhist Heaven. Still unpredictable and potentially dangerous, they are now regarded more as protectors of nature and punishers of human arrogance. They are also associated with an ascetic religion called Shugendo.

THREE-LEGGED CROW

As with many other East Asian mythical creatures, the three-legged crow originated in China and then spread into neighboring countries. This bird may be either a crow or a raven. Chinese legend also mentions a three-legged rooster, as well as an unspecified three-legged bird belonging to the goddess Xi Wangmu, Queen Mother of the West. These may or may not be alternative versions of the sanzuwu, the three-legged crow.

The sanzuwu is also known as yangwu or jinwu, the sun crow. It lives inside the sun. Its color is red or golden, rather than black like a normal crow. Chinese legend states that there used to be ten suns, each being home to a three-legged crow. At one point, all ten sun crows tried to descend to Earth, which would have caused the planet to burn up. The celestial archer Houyi saved the world by killing all but one of the birds.

The Japanese name for the three-legged crow is yatagarasu. Its name means "eight-span crow," meaning that it is large and divine. This bird is associated with Amaterasu, the goddess of the sun. The legendary first emperor of Japan, Jimmu, is said to have been guided by a yatagarasu across the country on the path toward his destiny. The bird is therefore a symbol of guidance and divine intervention in Japan.

In Korea, the three-legged crow is called samjoko. Also associated with the sun, it was historically considered the highest ranking of all mythical creatures. It was an especially important symbol in the ancient kingdoms of Goguryeo and the Joseon dynasty. Its image persists on various emblems and logos in Korea today.

USHI-ONI

The ushi-oni, or gyuki, is a highly varied class of yokai prevalent in western Japan. The word *ushi* means ox or cow. This label is applied to many dissimilarly shaped monsters, with their common characteristic being a bovine head. They are also usually associated with water. Some ushi-oni have humanoid bodies, while others are more bestial. Sometimes the name *ushi-oni* is reserved for marine types, while *gyuki* refers

to inland freshwater types. These creatures are typically feared predators. However, the ushi-oni is notably celebrated in Uwajima, where it symbolizes the Japanese victory over Korea in the Second Siege of Jinju in 1593.

Perhaps the most infamous ushi-oni is the one from northern Kyushu and western Honshu. This horrific horned beast has the body of an enormous spider. It is usually depicted with six legs rather than eight. Inhabiting the sea near the shore, this monster is often accompanied by female yokai, the nure-onna and the vampire-like iso-onna. These yokai seduce their victims and lure them to the water's edge, where the ushi-oni then leaps out and slaughters its prey.

A statue of a very different-looking ushi-oni stands at the Negoro-ji temple in the Wakayama Prefecture. This fiend is bipedal, with bulging eyes, long tusks, and terrible claws. It is covered with feathers, with large arms appearing to serve as wings. A plaque near the statue explains that this ushi-oni came out of the sea during the seventeenth century and terrorized a nearby village. The evil beast was vanquished by a great archer named Yamada Kurando Takakiyo. Its horns are still kept inside the temple today.

XIANGLIU

M ost Chinese mythical creatures are benevolent, yet one prominent exception is Xiangliu ("Shyong Lyoo"). Also called Minister Liu, this extremely powerful monster was an enormous green serpent with nine heads. These heads had human faces, according to the *Classic of Mountains and Seas*. Xiangliu was unbelievably large. His heads were able to devour prey from nine different mountaintops at the same time. He was so vile that his drool poisoned the land. Wherever he touched, the soil would rot and turn into foul-smelling swamps.

Xiangliu was the loyal servant and officer of a water god named Gong Gong. This being is also described as a monster, half human and half snake. Xiangliu once aided Gong Gong in a battle against the sky god, Zhuan Xu. They destroyed a great mountain that was holding up the sky and unleashed floods and mayhem onto the world. The floods were stopped by a legendary emperor named Yu the Great, who supposedly lived from 2200 to 2100 BCE. Yu is one of the great heroes of world mythology. Riding into battle on a dragon named Ying, he drove away Gong Gong and then was able to kill Xiangliu.

Unfortunately, when he sliced Xiangliu open, the monster's blood created a second flood. Yu made three attempts to bury or cover the toxic blood, yet to no avail. Finally he reshaped the land, digging great channels and building terraces. He built one high terrace dedicated to the gods, and then got onto it and prayed, thanking them for his successes in battle. The blood then drained from the land, and Yu founded the Xia dynasty.

Chapter Ten

THE PACIFIC

The Pacific Islands, as defined in this chapter, encompass all of Polynesia, Melanesia, Micronesia, Australia, and the Philippines. This region is also often referred to as Oceania, although the Philippines is usually not included under this label. Among the many Pacific Island cultural groups, the Polynesians are by far the most geographically spread out. Ancient Polynesians were the first people in the world to navigate the Pacific Ocean. They settled in New Zealand and on Easter Island, Hawaii, and many other islands. The second-most-widespread group is the Melanesians, whose homelands include Papua New Guinea, the Solomon Islands, and Fiji. Over 800 languages are spoken in Papua New Guinea, the most out of any country in the world.

In general, the Pacific Islands tend to be underrepresented in books about mythical creatures. This reflects their relative isolation from Western civilization, not an absence of culture and mythology. Seven mythical creatures in this chapter come from Australia. These represent Aboriginal beliefs as well as Western postcolonial folklore. The Philippines is a treasure trove of fantastical creatures as well. It contributes six entries to this book, while numerous other monsters can be found in Philippine folklore. Philippine myths reflect influence from a diverse range of sources, including many indigenous tribes, Southeast Asia, and Spanish culture. Another seven creatures in this chapter come from Polynesia, while the remaining four are from Melanesia.

ADARNA BIRD

The magical Adarna bird appears in a lengthy fairy tale epic from the Philippines titled *Ibong Adarna*. This staple of classic Philippine literature is believed to have been written by the poet José de la Cruz sometime during the eighteenth century. The author was educated by Spanish Jesuits, as Spain had conquered and colonized the Philippines during the eighteenth century. This uniquely Philippine fairy tale thus shows influence from traditional European folklore. The mythical Adarna bird is said to have rainbow feathers that shimmer like iridescent metal and a song of seven melodies with transformative powers. When King Fernando of the fictional kingdom of Berbania fell ill, the Adarna bird was the only being that could cure him.

Ibong Adarna chronicles the adventures of Don Juan, the youngest of King Fernando's three sons, who started out on a quest to find the Adarna bird. Throughout the book, Juan's efforts become hampered by his two unscrupulous brothers, Don Pedro and Don Diego. Early on in the story, the Adarna bird put the two elder brothers to sleep with its song. It then turned them into stone with its magical droppings. The two brothers are later brought back to life and continue to conspire against Juan, even after the bird cures their father. The remainder of the story details additional adventures of Don Juan. Eventually the Adarna bird returns to tell him that he should marry the princess Maria Blanca. This princess has magical talismans that she uses to aid Juan in his journeys and prove her love for him. In the end, Don Juan and Maria Blanca become wed.

ADARO MATAWA

The adaros are a class of malevolent spirits from the Solomon Islands, which are part of Melanesia. The adaro matawa, or *adaro ni matawa*, is a subclass of adaros resembling fish-people. They actually live in the sky, despite being sea spirits. They may use rainbows or water spouts as passages to travel to Earth. Normally invisible, adaro matawas are envisioned as humanoid with fins and other fish-like characteristics. They typically have features of larger fish species, such as swordfish, sawfish, and sharks. Some artists depict them as having a whole fish for a head, fish for feet, and other fish attached to their body. Many individual adaro matawas were known by name in traditional folklore. Their leader is named Ngoriaru.

Adaro matawas are dangerous beings, personifying forces of nature that humans cannot control. They are known to spontaneously attack humans by shooting invisible poisonous fish from a bow, like arrows. Fishermen may be struck by these fish in the neck or back, causing sudden pain, broken bones, and sickness. They will not see the fish but will experience the injury. The victim must consult a medicine priest to be healed. Adaro matawas are also occasionally known to seize control of humans via spirit possession.

More frequently, however, they control the weather at sea rather than harming people. The Solomon Islanders regard the adaro matawas with fear but also revere them. Sometimes these beings appear to people in dreams and teach them new songs and dances. Ghosts of dead people are also called adaros. Most adaro matawas are not dead people, but some are, as the Solomon Islanders traditionally buried their dead at sea.

ASWANG

Throughout the Philippines there are tales of horrible flesh-eating monsters called aswangs, or asuangs. These beings appear human by day and may blend in with other members of society. They can also disguise themselves as animals. At night they assume their true form and search for human flesh. Usually they are imagined as human-like with fangs, sharp claws, and a pair of leathery wings. In some regions they are described differently. These creatures feed on human corpses or on freshly killed victims. Most aswangs crave the human liver as their favorite food, although some eat fetuses stolen from their mothers' wombs. In some myths a person can become an aswang by eating human flesh.

There are many different kinds of aswang throughout the Philippines, reflecting the folkloric diversity of different indigenous cultures. Some Filipinos claim that the aswang is often accompanied by a demonic bird called the tik-tik or wak-wak, named for the sound it makes. Alternatively, the tik-tik is a type of aswang that transforms into a large bird or bat and preys on unborn babies. A prominent subclass of the aswang is called the manananggal. This monster appears by day as an attractive middle-aged woman. At night her torso separates from her lower body, sprouts wings, and flies about the village in search of fetuses to eat. The manananggal leaves her lower body standing up in her home. If this is found, a person should sprinkle salt, garlic, or ground onion onto its top. This prevents the manananggal's upper half from being able to reattach, forcing it to die at sunrise.

BAKUNAWA

Bakunawa is a great sea monster from the indigenous mythology of the Philippines. Modern Filipinos have conflated this being with the Asian or European dragon, but he was originally said to be shark-like or fish-like. This massive beast has a mouth as large as a lake and is sometimes depicted with four gray wings, a large pair and a small pair. He is the lord of the underworld, called Kasanaan, which is located at the bottom of the sea.

The native Tagalog people consider him to be the enemy of the sky god, Bathala. Among the Bicolanos he is the enemy of the moon goddess Haliya. In both versions, Bakunawa is infamous for his habit of leaping out of the water and attempting to devour the moon. This is the traditional explanation for lunar eclipses. According to some myths, Bakunawa is drawn to the moon because of its beauty. In others, he seeks to devour it out of revenge. In one myth, he despises humans because they killed a sea turtle who was his sister.

Historically, the Tagalogs believed that the god Bathala originally placed seven moons in the night sky. Bakunawa devoured six of them and was intending to swallow the seventh, until the people begged Bathala to intervene. Bathala instructed the people to cause a great commotion by banging loudly on pots and pans. The loud noise would disturb Bakunawa and cause him to spit the moon back out. To this day, the sea monster still sometimes attempts to devour the remaining moon, and people must bang on pots and pans to drive him away.

BUNYIP

The bunyip is one of the most well-known mythical creatures from Australia. The word *bunyip*, or *banip*, originally came from the Wemba-Wemba Aborigines of southeastern Australia. It seemingly referred to a terrifying supernatural being whose appearance was not specified. Other Aboriginal peoples had their own words for generic monsters and evil spirits. Westerners first assumed that all of these referred to the same creature. This reflects Europeans' historical ignorance about the complexity of Aboriginal culture. In the 1850s, Anglo-Australians used the word *bunyip* to mean humbug or fakery. They produced satirical cartoon monsters to depict this concept.

Before long, however, white Australians began seeing bunyips for themselves. Hundreds of people reported bunyip sightings throughout the nineteenth and early twentieth centuries. Descriptions of the monster were as inconsistent among Anglo-Australians as they were among Aboriginal societies. Sightings became so profuse in 1890 that officials from the Melbourne Zoo mounted an expedition to capture the beast. In actuality, many sightings are thought to have been seals and sea lions that swam upriver. Other descriptions suspiciously resembled swimming dogs. Some witnesses compared the beast to a horse, a camel, a hippo, or virtually any other animal.

Over time, the bunyip came to be imagined as a large, four-legged aquatic mammal with webbed feet, claws, and tusks. It is presumed to be dangerous. Images of the creature have appeared on Australian postage stamps and other media. Although sightings have more or less ceased, there remain some individuals who believe that the bunyip is or was a genuine cryptid species. Some cryptozoology enthusiasts suggest that it may be a surviving Diprotodon or other prehistoric mammal.

DROP BEAR

The drop bear is a contemporary Australian myth that did not originate among the Aborigines. It is neither a cryptid nor a part of any spiritual belief system but instead is regarded with humor. The drop bear is not a true bear, but a marsupial closely related to the koala. It is an exclusive carnivore named for its habit of dropping down onto its prey from above. It is specifically said to target tourists and people who do not speak with an Australian accent.

The Australian Museum in Sydney maintains an official profile on the drop bear, which can be found on the museum's website. It names the species scientifically as *Thylarctos plummettus*. The adult drop bear weighs 120 kilograms (260 pounds). It is 130 centimeters (51 inches) long and 90 centimeters (3 feet) high at the shoulder. Its color is orange.

Fortunately, there are a number of ways one can avoid being attacked by a drop bear. It is thought that drop bears not only recognize Australian accents, but they also dislike the smell of Vegemite exuded in Australian sweat. A tourist can therefore repel drop bears by smearing the yeast-based paste on the back of their neck, behind their ears, and in their armpits. Toothpaste may substitute for Vegemite, and urinating in one's pants may also deter the creature. Some Australian tour guides recommend that travelers wear upward-pointing forks in their hair. A person can test whether a tree harbors a drop bear by spitting straight up into the air. If the animal is present, it will spit back down at them.

FIGONA

The figonas are a supernatural race that was once worshipped by the native Melanesians of the Solomon Islands. These beings are primordial nature spirits that protect sacred groves, waters, and other natural sites. They are intangible like ghosts and often live inside stones and other natural objects. Although they are normally invisible to the human eye, figonas are envisioned as giant snakes.

Their leader is named Agunua or Hatuibwari. This figure was historically considered a god. He could take the form of a gigantic winged serpent, sometimes with a human head. In some regions he was said to appear as a man with a snake's tail. Some said that he had four eyes. Some said he had breasts like a woman and was able to nurse all the people whom he created. Agunua is credited with shaping the terrain and teaching the first humans how to plant and cook. Aside from Agunua, most figonas that appear in legends are female. They are shaped like regular snakes but behave like people.

Traditional stories describe a time when these beings frequently interacted with humans. Historically, the Solomon Islanders would leave them offerings of food and recite chants and prayers. The islanders did not confuse ordinary snakes with figonas, as most of the local snakes are venomous and are often killed on sight. In contrast, the figonas were sacred beings. They had human-like flaws but were considered benevolent. Yet, with the introduction of Christianity to the Solomon Islands, the native Melanesians eventually adopted the idea that all snakes are evil, including figonas. Many Solomon Islanders are now ashamed of their former beliefs.

HOKIOI

Giant birds once inhabited New Zealand, and although they are now extinct, they still appear in Maori myth and legend. The hokioi may have been inspired by the Haast's eagle, *Harpagornis moorei*, which became extinct in the 1400s. An exaggerated version of this giant eagle survives in myth as the human-eating pouakai. The relationship between the pouakai and the hokioi is unclear, although they are often considered separate species in myth. As with the pouakai, the hokioi is a giant bird of prey, and

the Maori believe it to have been real at one time. Yet, unlike any real bird, each of the hokioi's wings is said to have four joints. It is predominantly black and white, with yellow and green highlights, and a large red crest atop its head.

One folktale states that the hokioi once entered a competition against a hawk to see who could fly the highest. The hawk became overpowered by gusts of wind or, alternatively, was distracted by the sight of mice on the ground. The hokioi continued to race upward until it exited the visible sky and could no longer see the Earth below. Because of this, the legendary bird lives at heights unseen by mortals.

Some Maori believe that the hokioi lived up on the highest mountains. Others say it lived in the celestial realm as the companion of Hine-Whaitiri, the goddess of thunder. Only at night would it descend low enough for people to hear its call, "Hokioi, hokioi, hu-u." This call was considered an ill omen. Some believe that this call actually belonged to a real nocturnal bird that has not been identified.

KAUPE

A popular Hawaiian ghost story concerns a dreadful phantom named Kaupe, a magical human-dog shapeshifter who lived long ago. His ghost is said to look like a large humanoid with a dog's head and claws. He can also assume the form of a vicious dog with a taste for human flesh. This ghost is often spotted in the Nu'uanu Valley in Oahu, where Kaupe originated, or under the bridge in Kipapa Gulch, where many ghosts are sighted. According to folklore, he will create sounds of people crying out in pain and terror. When a passerby checks for the source of the sound, they will see Kaupe slinking off into the darkness.

Kaupe was the villain of a legend taking place in an ancient kingdom on the island of Oahu. The evil *kupua*, or supernatural being, one day materialized on the island. Before long he laid the kingdom to waste. He would often lie in wait as fishermen walked home at night, whereupon he would ambush them, maul them to death, and devour their flesh.

Eventually he expanded his bloody rampage to the islands of Maui and Hawaii. When on the big island of Hawaii, he abducted a young man of the chiefly *ali'i* caste and brought him back to Oahu. Kaupe held the young nobleman prisoner at his temple to sacrifice him to his dark gods. The young man's father traveled to Oahu and, with the aid of the kingdom's top priest, managed to rescue his son. Kaupe pursued them back to Hawaii, where a war ensued. The people were able to kill him using prayers they learned from the priest.

KWAHALA

G oodenough Island, also called Nidula by its Melanesian inhabitants, is located off the east coast of Papua New Guinea. The people of Nidula have a strong belief in sorcery. The kwahala is a common supernatural familiar that sorcerers can control. It looks like a bird with horrible talons and a beak designed for tearing. It is luminous on the inside, the light being visible where its wings meet its breast. This light flickers at night as the creature flaps its wings. Its droppings glow like fireflies. The kwahala is also compared to a large bat, as bats are classified as birds in the indigenous language. It may have bat-like wings and fly with bat-like movements. It reeks like rotting flesh and is often only smelled rather than seen.

Sorcerers summon and control kwahalas using special mystical stones. The sorcerer is magically sustained when the bird eats, as the kwahala is essentially an extension of himself. If the bird is killed, the sorcerer also dies. Kwahalas are known to desecrate graves in order to feed on human corpses. The sorcerer may also send the kwahala to attack living people. The bird will tear out the victims' insides, yet will do so only magically, without cutting their flesh visibly. The victim is not initially aware of the attack but quickly falls ill.

One particularly infamous sorcerer named Tobowa lived during the twentieth century. He once set a kwahala upon his wife because he felt she did not share enough food with him. Later, another sorcerer named Kimaola swore to put an end to Tobowa. He succeeded in killing Tobowa after deploying a flock of kwahalas.

MANAIA

The manaia is one of many motifs that appears in traditional Maori art from New Zealand. A highly stylized creature, it looks like an abstract design at first glance. Upon closer inspection, one can see that it has a beak like a bird, and a long, curling, serpentine body. Its body is variously thought to be that of a snake, a lizard, or a seahorse, and it may be imagined to have a human torso. Oftentimes it has one arm visible. It may also have a fish-like tail or other decorative features. As a standard, the manaia is always depicted in profile. It is believed to be a protective symbol. Shaped like a figure-eight, it often appears on houses, wooden posts, weapons, and jewelry to ward off evil.

The origin of the manaia is unclear, but it may be related to similar symbols from other Polynesian cultures. Unlike most mythical creatures, it is not known to play a role in any specific legend or story. Instead, art historians believe that the manaia is simply an artistic component used for constructing more elaborate images. Stylized humanoid and supernatural beings in Maori art are often composed of two manaias facing each other. It seemingly began as an artistic design first and became a mythical creature second. The word *manaia* may be derived from the Samoa word *fa'amanaia*, which means "to decorate." Manaia was also the name of an ancestral chief from Maori legend. New Zealanders today recognize this motif as a type of imaginary animal. It is one of the most prevalent images in Maori art.

MANANANGGAL

—See *Aswang*.

MULDJEWANGK

The muldjewangk comes from the folklore of the Ngarrindjeri Aborigines along the Murray River in Australia, especially near Lake Alexandrina. The Aborigines did not provide a specific description of the creature's appearance. Sometimes it is imagined as a huge aquatic ogre or giant grotesque merman, while other times it is assumed to be a serpentine creature. Sources also differ over whether there is more than one muldjewangk. Despite these inconsistencies, the monster is always regarded with fear. Ngarrindjeri parents used to tell their children that the muldjewangk will grab them if they go too close to the river after dark. If the creature grabs a child, a shaman can possibly go rescue him or her, but this is very difficult to do. The muldjewangk also appears in Ngarrindjeri Dreamtime stories as an antagonist who ruins people's fishing nets.

One Aboriginal anecdote recounts a muldjewangk attacking a steamboat that was towing three barges in the Murray River. The giant monster grabbed hold of the steamboat and stopped it right in its course. The people onboard saw its enormous hands grasping the hull. Immediately the captain reached for his gun. There were Aboriginal elders onboard and they warned the captain not to shoot. The captain did not listen to them and shot the monster dead. Still, it clung to the boat. The people had to cut the steamboat loose, abandon ship, and let the boat sink to the bottom of the river. There was also another consequence: the captain quickly fell ill. His body erupted in weeping red blisters all over, and he soon died from the mysterious disease.

PONATURI

The folklore of Polynesia and other Pacific cultures includes various races of magical humanoid beings. The ponaturi are one of the more monstrous of these. This race dwells in the dark underworld at the bottom of the sea near New Zealand. These evil humanoids have ghastly white skin and hair the color of fresh blood. Their most fearsome feature is their claws, with which they rend the flesh from their victims' bones. Occasionally the ponaturi come ashore in search of human prey. They travel in large hordes. These creatures abhor bright light and will only emerge onto land at night.

Some Maori legends describe epic battles between humans and ponaturi. One story concerns a legendary hero named Rata. One night, this hero discovered that the ponaturi had stolen the bones of his deceased father, Wahieroa, who was also a great warrior. Rata spied a group of ponaturi sorcerers using the bones for witchcraft. They uttered the words of a spell, trying to curse Rata. But Wahieroa's bones would not harm his son. Rata managed to kill the sorcerers and take the bones.

The ponaturi returned for revenge the following night. But Rata was prepared for battle. He had his warriors ready and was carrying Wahieroa's bones in a pouch at his side. Unfortunately, the ponaturi greatly outnumbered the Maori warriors. Before long, Rata was one of the only men still standing. Suddenly, Wahieroa's bones began to shake. His spirit was reminding his son of the spell he had heard the night before. Upon this reminder, Rata chanted the spell. His fallen warriors magically returned to life and defeated the entire ponaturi army.

RAINBOW SERPENT

The Rainbow Serpent is the most widely known mythical creature from Australia. It may also be the oldest known mythical creature in the world, as it is depicted in rock art dating back at least 6,000 years. The Rainbow Serpent is almost universal among approximately 500 Aboriginal cultures. This enormous, colorful snake is a sacred being who roamed the Earth in the primordial time and space known as the Dreaming, or Dreamtime. It is associated with creation, fertility, water, and rain. In many stories it is both a creator and a destroyer. Rainbows are thought to be either symbols or actual manifestations of the Rainbow Serpent in the majority of tribes.

There is much variability between Rainbow Serpent myths. Usually the creature is considered male, but to some tribes it is female. In Arnhem Land there are many Rainbow Serpents, which are called *bolung*. The same word also refers to an actual rainbow. A bolung can enter a woman's body to become a developing fetus, and after a person's death, their soul becomes a bolung once again. More broadly, Rainbow Serpents are known from myths that explain how the features of the land came into existence. Some stories describe how the serpent taught culture to early humans. In many myths it embodies the chaotic and unpredictable forces of nature. For instance, a Bundjalung myth from eastern Australia describes a time when the Rainbow Serpent posed a great threat to the world. A shaman named Nyimbunji summoned a giant monitor lizard named Dirawong, who fought against the Rainbow Serpent and banished it to the bottom of the sea.

ROPEN

The ropen originated in Papua New Guinea, its name coming from the locality of Umboi Island. Yet, rather than being a strictly Melanesian myth, this creature has also entered the folklore of Westerners in Australia and the United States. According to the Western interpretation, the ropen is a living pterosaur or pterodactyl. Other flying monsters are known in Papua New Guinea by various names. Some cryptozoologists believe that all of these are the same species, and apply the name *ropen* to all of them.

Unfortunately, little has been recorded regarding the indigenous Papuan beliefs about the ropen. The bits and pieces collected suggest an animal that may be similar to the kwahala, albeit much larger. The ropen is said to feed on fish and carrion and will sometimes rob graves to eat human corpses. It is also bioluminescent. Papuans from Umboi Island associate this creature with mysterious lights in the sky that they call *indava*.

Most written material about the ropen is geared toward cryptozoology enthusiasts. This creature is especially popular among a particular faction of Christian fundamentalist cryptozoologists. Spearheaded by Young Earth Creationists, this group seeks out living pterosaurs and dinosaurs in hopes of overturning scientific doctrine. Their writings allege that the ropen has a wingspan of 20 to 50 feet. It has a long crest on its head, as well as a 15-foot-long tail ending in a diamond-shaped vane. This combination of features does not occur in any known fossil pterosaur, yet it resembles the popular portrayal of pterosaurs in cartoons. The enthusiasm of Western pterosaur hunters has probably influenced the Umboi natives' perception of the ropen, yet it is unclear to what extent.

RURUHI-KEREPO

Ruruhi-Kerepo is the name of a horrible ogress from Maori folklore in New Zealand. Her name means "blind old woman." She is able to appear as a harmless elderly woman, seemingly helpless with her disability of blindness. In actuality she possesses incredible strength. She can leap distances so great that she appears to be flying. Her hands are large and hairy and armed with sharp talons. She can unhinge her jaws to an extraordinary gape, revealing scores of pointed teeth. Most infamously of all, Ruruhi-Kerepo's body is covered with sharp spines. These spines are the splintered bones of her victims, which protrude through her flesh after she devours them.

One day, a group of five teenage girls encountered what they thought was a feeble old woman. Young and irreverent, the girls mocked her old age. The woman sweetly told them not to call her "old woman," but "aunt." The girls felt ashamed and apologized. Ruruhi-Kerepo then invited them to a contest to see which girl could climb a tree the highest. All the girls climbed the tree until they could not get back down. Ruruhi-Kerepo then reached up with her monstrous hands, pulled one of the girls down, and devoured her. Meanwhile, a search party of warriors went out looking for the girls. Unfortunately, they arrived too late, as all five girls had been eaten. The warriors tried to beat Ruruhi-Kerepo with their clubs, but the fresh bones protruding from her skin served as armor. Ruruhi-Kerepo lashed back at the warriors with her claws. The men switched their weapons from clubs to spears and were then able to kill her.

SIGBIN

The dreaded sigbin is one of the Philippines' most nightmarish mythical creatures. This relatively small supernatural beast looks like a hornless goat, yet with certain unnatural characteristics. It has extremely large ears, which it can clap together like hands to produce a loud noise. According to some descriptions, it also has a long tail that it can use as a whip. It is sometimes said to walk backward, with its head lowered to the ground, looking behind from between its legs. The sigbin is usually invisible in the daytime. The presence of this creature can be detected by a nauseating odor. When seen, it usually appears as a flitting shadow.

Sigbins prey on humans and other animals by attacking their shadow. The victim may not be aware of the attack but will suddenly fall seriously ill. Sigbins are attracted to the sick and the dying. They will linger around a dying person and sleep underneath the person's house. After the person has died, it will continue to linger for nine days, the duration of the Catholic novena for the dead. Sigbins also eat squash blossoms and occasionally coal.

It is thought that sigbins are owned by people called *sigbinan*. These individuals are witches and sorcerers who keep their evil pets in clay jars. They may have several of them. During Holy Week, sigbinan may send out their familiars to retrieve the hearts of children, which they fashion into magical amulets. To this day there are many Filipinos who believe in the existence of sigbins, especially in rural areas of the Visayas Islands and Mindanao.

SIYOKOY

Filipino folklore includes multiple classes of merfolk known broadly as Bantay-Tubig. The siyokoy is the most grotesque variety. Siyokoy are generally described as being covered with scales and having sharp teeth. Beyond this, there is no single standard description of their form. They are depicted varyingly as human-shaped or merman-shaped. Some contemporary artists embellish them with other monstrous features, such as tentacles. They are usually thought to have hideous fish-like faces and webbed hands and feet.

Siyokoy are able to walk on land, but only for a short time before they risk death by dehydration. They are also able to shapeshift into humans, usually handsome men, to seduce women and impregnate them. They are also believed to have power over the weather at sea. Among the Waray people, the siyokoy are called ugkoy and live in fresh water. All siyokoy are male. Their female counterparts are called sirena, which are mermaids like those in European folklore. Even their name is of European origin. A third class of Bantay-Tubig is the kataw, or catao. They, too, are more human-like in appearance than the siyokoy.

In general, the Bantay-Tubig are enemies of humankind, or more accurately, they see humans as enemies of the ocean world. Siyokoys' encounters with humans often involve them dragging humans underwater by their feet to drown them. They have even been blamed for sinking ships. Despite their monstrous form, the siyokoy are intelligent and civilized, often adorning themselves with shells and other ornaments. They are regarded as benevolent in their underwater kingdom, serving the role of leaders and protectors of undersea animal life.

TANGATA-MANU

Rapa Nui, also known as Easter Island, is the home of Tangata-Manu or "Bird Man." This island once supported a Polynesian civilization that built the famous *moai* statues. Tangata-Manu became a prominent symbol of Rapa Nui's religion and culture sometime after the statues stopped being built. This motif is associated with

the worship of a benevolent fertility god named Makemake. It is probably not a depiction of Makemake himself, but more likely a subordinate being who serves him. Tagata-Manu is normally depicted holding an egg. His head has been identified as that of a frigatebird, a distinctive species known for its remarkable investment in parenting. Some of the islanders claim that the Tangata-Manu were a race that built the moai.

Historically, Rapa Nui natives used to hold an annual festival in honor of Tangata-Manu. It involved a competition at a site called Orongo, whose cliffs overlook the smaller island of Motu Nui. Motu Nui used to be the nesting site of seabirds, especially the sooty tern. Clan leaders would each send a servant to swim out to Motu Nui to retrieve the first tern's egg of the season. The first egg laid each year was believed to contain the essence of Makemake. Once the servant collected an egg, he would swim back with it and scale the cliffs back up to Orongo. The master of the winning servant was crowned honorary Bird Man. He would carve a new image of Tangata-Manu onto the rocks at Orongo and then move off to a special retreat. There he would be treated as a living god for a year.

TANIWHA

Arguably the most famous mythical creature in New Zealand, the taniwha may also be the most prominent monster in all of Polynesia. The Maori people tell countless tales of these gigantic, ferocious, intelligent beasts. Few generalizations apply to all taniwhas. Many of them resemble gargantuan lizards or lizard-like reptiles, although some look more like sharks. They are powerful and dangerous and some are ravenous for human flesh. Others are more reserved and some are actually benevolent. The majority of taniwhas dwell in water, yet some live on land. Some burrow underground and some can even fly. Some can change their shape. A large percentage of the taniwhas are descendants of the god Tane and the mountain spirit Hine-Tupari-Maunga. Some are the reincarnated souls of human ancestors.

Many features and phenomena of the natural world are attributed to the acts of taniwhas. These gigantic creatures have the ability to create lakes and whirlpools and upend the land itself. The Maori believe that certain large boulders are actually the bodies of retired taniwhas, which are still charged with the creatures' spiritual power. According to some stories, lizards exist because small pieces of taniwhas escaped when the relentless monsters were being burned to death by humans. A benevolent taniwha named Horomatangi created the Horomatangi Reef and other landmarks in order to guide the Maori ancestors to New Zealand from afar. An ocean-dwelling taniwha named Parata is responsible for the tides. Parata is so massive that he causes the tides to ebb by drawing water into his enormous mouth. The tides climb back to the shore as he closes his mouth and expels the water.

TIKBALANG

The tikbalang is one of the better-known mythical creatures from the Philippines. It is a class of magical spirit that lives in the forest, especially in nipa groves, in banyan trees, and near hot springs. It is usually described as a tall humanoid with the head and legs of a horse. Some descriptions give this race extremely long limbs and horrible teeth. They have the ability to shapeshift into humans and other animals.

Tikbalangs are considered mischievous and sometimes downright evil. These creatures have been blamed for human abduction, rape, cursing people with illness, and occasionally murder. Yet, more often than attacking humans physically, tikbalangs are known to confuse people walking through the woods. They may cause travelers to become lost and go mad, although the effect of this magic is usually temporary. The tikbalang was probably viewed more favorably prior to missionization by the Spaniards. One early Augustinian priest complained that the indigenous Filipinos would befriend the tikbalang and surrender their rosaries to it, in exchange for magical charms and favors.

Tikbalangs are nature spirits that protect the forest. According to some, an individual can pass through a grove unmolested simply by asking for permission first. A tikbalang may even befriend a human, in which case it will greet its ally by calling, "Tik-tik!" Each tikbalang is believed to carry a magical stone, called a *mutya*, which humans may possess if they ride on its back. These creatures can be tamed like regular horses. To tame one, a person must pluck out one of the three stiffest hairs from its mane and make a talisman out of the hair.

WAHWEE

The Wahwee is a water monster from various Aboriginal cultures of New South Wales, Australia. It is serpentine with a frog-like head and six legs. The creature dwells in large waterholes, particularly in the muddy banks, in which it carves out deep tunnels and dens. People must exercise utmost caution and respect while collecting shellfish and other items from these waterholes. The Wahwee is a carnivore and will sometimes prey on humans. It also possesses formidable supernatural powers. It wields command over water and rain and can produce floods and droughts. It is also capable of shapeshifting. Shamans may visit the Wahwee to learn new songs and ceremonies for their people.

One story tells of a teenage girl named Nerida who liked to collect shellfish from the Wahwee's waterhole. Other members of the village repeatedly warned her not to do that, yet she took no heed. One day, she met an old woman at the waterhole who was sobbing. The old woman told her that, due to Nerida's selfishness, the Wahwee would unleash a flood upon the village, killing everyone. Nerida felt terrible. She said she would rather sacrifice herself than put her village in danger. She did not know that the old woman was actually the Wahwee. The woman instructed her to meet her at the waterhole the next day. Nerida went as told and was never seen again. Soon, her boyfriend visited the waterhole and called out to her. A beautiful red lily appeared on the surface of the water. The boy then dove into the water and became a water rush. The waterhole became lush with lilies and rushes.

YARA-MA-YHA-WHO

The yara-ma-yha-who is a peculiar little Australian monster generally attributed to Aboriginal folklore. It is a nursery bogey, serving the purpose of instilling children with fear. The creature is 3 feet tall, frog-like, bipedal, and red in color. It has small limbs, a pot belly, a large head, and a huge, toothless mouth. Some artists depict the creature as being hairy. Perhaps most unusual of all, it has a set of suckers attached to its fingertips and toes, which it uses to suck out people's blood. The yara-ma-yha-who dwells in the foliage of fig trees. If a person stops to rest under a fig tree, the creature will drop down on top of them and begin sucking their blood with its fingers.

Parents advise children to remain still if they are ever attacked by a yara-ma-yha-who. The monster continues sucking its victim's blood for as long as the victim keeps moving. When the victim stops moving, the yara-ma-yha-who swallows them whole. It then takes a nap, and when it awakens, it drinks water from a pond and regurgitates its meal. The victim comes out alive and unscathed but is a little bit smaller than they were before, and a little bit redder in color. The yara-ma-yha-who then seeks to repeat the process over again, but only if it knows its victim is still alive. For this reason, parents advise children to play dead. Children may successfully escape if the creature is fooled. Yet, if the child is swallowed and regurgitated many times, they become a yara-ma-yha-who. Once changed, they become magically bound to the fig tree.

YOWIE

The yowie is a large, fur-covered humanoid with beast-like features. A blend of Australian Aboriginal and Anglo-Australian folklore, the legend of this creature continues to evolve in the present day. It is similar in many ways to Sasquatch of North America. Many Australians believe in its existence, and some presume it to be the same species as Sasquatch. But the yowie also has certain features that distinguish it from its North American counterpart. Behaviorally, it is considered more aggressive. Some artistic renderings portray the yowie with prominent fangs or tusks. Its feet are inconsistently described but are generally thought to be shaped differently from human feet. It may have only three or four toes on each foot, or its feet may point backward. Additionally, the yowie is frequently said to have large claws on its hands. Cryptozoology enthusiasts claim yowies mark their territory by leaving deep claw marks on trees.

The name "yowie" is thought by many to come from *youree* or *yuuri*, one of the Aboriginal names for the creature. It was also formerly known as the yahoo until the 1970s. Many Australians think this name is of Aboriginal origin, yet it is a suspicious coincidence that "Yahoo" was a race of ape-like humanoids from *Gulliver's Travels* by Jonathan Swift. Ample evidence supports an Aboriginal origin of the creature, although its description seems to have transformed over time. Aboriginal descriptions are not all consistent with one another, nor are they consistent with the contemporary, scientifically inspired conception of an ape-like hominid. Older versions often overlapped with the bunyip and were subject to individual interpretation.

SELECTED BIBLIOGRAPHY

Afanas'ev, Aleksander. 1973. *Russian Fairy Tales*. Translated by Norbert Guterman. New York: Random House.

Almario, Virgilio S. 2001. *Ibong Adarna: A Book in 2 Languages*. Quezon City, The Philippines: Adarna House.

Ashton, John. 2012. *Curious Creatures in Zoology*. London: Forgotten Books.

Barnouw, Victor. 1977. *Wisconsin Chippewa Myths and Tales and Their Relation to Chippewa Life*. Madison: University of Wisconsin Press.

Birrell, Anne. 2000. *Chinese Myths*. Austin: University of Texas Press.

Borges, Jorge Luis. 2005. *The Book of Imaginary Beings*. Translated by Andrew Hurley. New York: Penguin Group.

Carey, Bjorn. 2011. "El Chupacabra Mystery Solved: A Case of Mistaken Identity." *LiveScience*, March 22, 2011. Accessed February 25, 2015. www.livescience. com/13356-el-chupacabra-mystery-solved.html.

Coldiron, Margaret. 2005. "Lions, Witches, and Happy Old Men: Some Parallels Between Balinese and Japanese Ritual Masks." *Asian Theatre Journal* 22, no. 2: 227–48.

Coleman, Loren, and Jerome Clark. 1999. *Cryptozoology A to Z: The Encyclopedia of Loch Monsters, Sasquatch, Chupacabras, and Other Authentic Mysteries of Nature*. New York: Fireside.

Colman, Narciso R. 1937. *Nuestros Antepasados (Nande Ypy Kuera)*. Virtual Library of Paraguay. Accessed October 8, 2014. www.portalguarani.com/376_narciso_ramon_ colman_rosicran_/10966_nuestros_antepasados_nande_ypy_kuera__obra_de_ narciso_r_colman_.html.

Curtis, Vesta Sarkhosh. 1993. *Persian Myths*. Austin: University of Texas Press.

Dalley, Stephanie, trans. 2008. *Myths from Mesopotamia: Creation, the Flood, Gilgamesh, and Others*. New York: Oxford University Press.

Dawood, N. J., trans. 2006. *The Voyages of Sindbad*. New York: Penguin Group.

Dixon-Kennedy, Mike. 1998. *Encyclopedia of Russian and Slavic Myth and Legend*. Santa Barbara, CA: ABC-CLIO.

Dorson, Richard Mercer. 1982. *Man and Beast in American Comic Legend*. Bloomington: Indiana University Press.

Ellis, Richard. 1994. *Monsters of the Sea*. New York: Alfred A. Knopf.

Ferdowsi, Abolqasem. 2007. *The Shahnameh: The Persian Book of Kings*. Translated by Dick Davis. New York: Penguin Classics.

Fox, C. E., and F. H. Drew. 1915. "Beliefs and Tales of San Cristoval." *Journal of the Royal Anthropological Institute of Great Britain and Ireland* 45: 187–228.

Freeman, Richard. 2010. *The Great Yokai Encyclopaedia: The A–Z of Japanese Monsters*. Bideford, UK: CFZ.

Gane, Constance Ellen. 2012. *Composite Beings in Neo-Babylonian Art*. PhD diss., Near Eastern Studies, University of California, Berkeley. https://escholarship.org/uc/ item/3p25f7wk#page-1 Accessed January 2, 2015.

Gill, Sam D., and Irene F. Sullivan. 1992. *Dictionary of Native American Mythology*. New York: Oxford University Press.

Hall, Clayton, and Jane Thomas, eds. 1997. *Chimney Pond Tales: Yarns Told by Leroy Dudley*. Cumberland Center, ME: Pamola.

Heuvelmans, Bernard. 1959. *On the Track of Unknown Animals*. Translated by Richard Garnet. London: Rupert Hart-Davis.

Heyerdahl, Thor. 1958. *Aku-Aku: The Secret of Easter Island*. Chicago: Rand McNally.

Homer. *The Odyssey of Homer*. Translated by Richmond Lattimore. New York: Harper Perennial Modern Classics, 2007.

Karnchanapayap, Yongkiat. 2013. *Himmapan*. E-book, accessed May 25, 2013. www.himmapan.com.

Knappert, Jan. 1977. *Bantu Myths and Other Tales*. Boston: Brill.

Kushnir, Dmitriy. 2014. *Creatures of Slavic Myth: The Slavic Way Volume 4*. CreateSpace Independent Publishing Platform.

Lang, Andrew. 1966. *The Violet Fairy Book*. New York: Dover.

Mack, Carol K., and Dinah Mack. 2011. *A Field Guide to Demons, Vampires, Fallen Angels, and Other Subversive Spirits*. New York: Henry Holt.

Mackal, Roy P. 1987. *A Living Dinosaur? In Search of the Mokele-Mbembe*. Boston: Brill.

Menon, Ramesh, trans. 2008. *The Ramayana: A Modern Translation*. New York: Harper Collins.

Miller, Mary, and Karl Taube. 1993. *An Illustrated Dictionary of the Gods and Symbols of Ancient Mexico and the Maya*. London: Thames & Hudson.

Murthy, K. Krishna. 1985. *Mythical Animals in Indian Art*. New Delhi: Shakti Malik.

Nigg, Joseph, ed. 1999. *The Book of Fabulous Beasts: A Treasury of Writings from Ancient Times to the Present*. New York: Oxford University Press.

Press, Petra. 1997. *Great Heroes of Mythology*. New York: MetroBooks.

Ramos, Maximo D. 1971. *Creatures of Philippine Lower Mythology*. Quezon City: University of the Philippines Press.

Reddish, Laura, and Orrin Lewis. 1998–2013. "Native American Figures of Myth and Legend." Native Languages of the Americas: Preserving and Promoting American Indian Languages. Accessed October 7, 2014. www.native-languages.org/legends-figures.htm

Reed, A. W. 1983. *Maori Myth and Legend*. Wellington, New Zealand. A. H. & A. W. Reed.

Rose, Carol. 2000. *Giants, Monsters, and Dragons: An Encyclopedia of Folklore, Legend, and Myth*. New York: W. W. Norton.

Roughsey, Dick. 1988. *The Rainbow Serpent*. Milwaukee, WI: Gareth Stevens.

Shepard, Odell. 1930. *The Lore of the Unicorn*. New York: Dover.

Shuker, Karl P. N. 2003. *The Beasts That Hide from Man: Seeking the World's Last Undiscovered Animals*. New York: ParaView.

———. 1995. *Dragons: A Natural History*. New York: Barnes & Noble Books.

Smith, Nigel. 1996. *The Enchanted Amazon Rain Forest*. Gainesville: University Press of Florida.

Strassberg, Richard E., trans. 2002. *A Chinese Bestiary: Strange Creatures from the Guideways through Mountains and Seas*. Berkeley: University of California Press.

Tedlock, Dennis, trans. 1996. *Popol Vuh: The Definitive Edition of the Mayan Book of the Dawn of Life and the Glories of Gods and Kings*. New York: Touchstone.

Werner, Alice. 1933. *Myths and Legends of the Bantu*. E-book, accessed March 23, 2016. www.sacred-texts.com/afr/mlb/index.htm

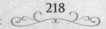

Westervelt, William Drake. 1987. *Myths and Legends of Hawaii*. Edited by A. Grove Day. Honolulu, HI: Mutual.

Whittall, Austin. 2012. *Monsters of Patagonia: A Guide to Its Giants, Dwarves, Lake Creatures and Mythical Beasts*. Buenos Aires, Argentina: Zagier & Urruty.

CREATURE INDEX